2013!

The Beginning
is Here

2013!

The Beginning is Here

Jim Young

BOOKS

Winchester, UK
Washington, USA

First published by O-Books, 2011
O-Books is an imprint of John Hunt Publishing Ltd., Laurel House, Station Approach,
Alresford, Hants, SO24 9JH, UK
office1@o-books.net
www.o-books.com

For distributor details and how to order please visit the 'Ordering' section on our website.

Text copyright: Jim Young 2010

ISBN: 978 1 84694 565 6

A CIP catalogue record for this book is available from the British Library.

Worldshift Movement (www.worldshiftmovement.org)
Worldshift Media (www.worldshiftmedia.org)

Design: Stuart Davies

Printed in the UK by CPI Antony Rowe
Printed in the USA by Offset Paperback Mfrs, Inc

We operate a distinctive and ethical publishing philosophy in all
areas of our business, from our global network of authors to
production and worldwide distribution.

CONTENTS

Acknowledgements

Along this journey we call life, experience has shown me that we are inspired or nudged to take action even when least expecting the need to do so. In this regard, there are many to thank for supporting this collection of viewpoints to consider when discerning our thoughts and feelings about the circumstances and conditions related to the end of the Mayan calendar on December 21, 2012.

Recently, Roland Emmerich's film, *2012*, caught my attention and ignited my passion to respond in some fashion. Although I was not happy about this challenge at first, I certainly am glad that I responded with the healthy sense of surrender I have learned to apply in other aspects of living from a spiritual perspective.

I thank my trustworthy friend and author in her own right, Marguerite Burgin, who first loaned me a book of articles on 2012, which further fanned the flames of enthusiasm for this project; and I thank her for her support and guidance since. I am also grateful for the editorial commentary suggested by my friend and talented author, Jenny Wagget.

I add to this my immense gratitude to each of the authors contributing to this anthology. They responded quickly and enthusiastically to the call for action. The significance of the content, as well as their commitment to quality, speak well of them. I also owe great thanks to Gareth Strangemore-Jones, of WorldShift Media, who, early on, committed to move this book out into the array of organizations and individuals collaborating with the WorldShift 2012 movement.

I give thanks, also, to several persons at O-Books: John Hunt, Publisher, who offered a quick and affirming hand in bringing this book to publication: Trevor Greenfield, for his skilled supervision of the publication process; Hayley Sherman, Copy Editor, whose remarkable editorial eye has given literary integrity to the final version; and Stuart Davies, Designer, for presenting the book in its best light. Singly, and as a team, these dedicated individuals have demonstrated their undying commitment to the highest quality publication.

I extend heartfelt thanks to Trudy Woodcock, Director of Casa K' and Illuminado Tours in Merida, MX, who translated Miguel Angel Vergara's chapter from Spanish into English as a contribution in faith.

Gratefully, this project has afforded me yet another opportunity to collaborate with a person I respect and admire as one of the most creative individuals I know: Todd Young, founder and chief officer of Todd Young Studio.com. Todd inspired the subtitle of the book and brilliantly created the cover design.

I also wish to thank family and friends, who have offered encouragement and interest along the way. You know who you are. Thank you, one and all.

Of late, I have come to appreciate the wide and deep interest in the potential for this book from the many who have participated in the presentations I've been making from the content of other spiritual books to come from me. Indeed, their excitement over the future availability of information and ideas related to 2012 has affirmed, yet again, the decision to carry this project forward to completion.

I greatly appreciate the endless array of inspirational imagery that stirs us deeply, affording us with opportunities to go inward yet again, so we can hone our inherent capacity for discerning the meaning of such appearances from a deeper place. And so we can join in lifting spiritual consciousness to its rightful place among and within us. Indeed, I thank the Spirit that guides me day-to-day, moment-to-moment. Without devoted attention to this inner Source, neither the inspiration to begin nor the commitment to see it through to the end would have prevailed. Once again, I have come to appreciate the simple act of showing up at the feet of inspiration, Wisdom, so she may show me the way…

Jim Young

Introduction

I don't suppose I need to tell you that the year 2012 is fast-approaching, and that there is great controversy over the end of the Mayan Calendar and related prophecies, as well as how these could affect planet Earth in that time period. My suspicion is that you are aware of the controversial nature of all this or you wouldn't be showing interest by beginning to read this book about it. I won't labor the introduction with excerpts from chapters contained in this compendium; you will be in the midst of the writings from various experts soon enough. Instead, I'd like you to have some semblance of understanding about how this book came about. If you've had no experience in such realms, this brief story may well be of interest, even encouraging. If you have published a book or books of your own, a story like this one can still be inspiring.

Some time ago, while attending a movie, the trailer for the Roland Emmerich film, *2012*, came onto the screen. I was outraged at the highly disoriented and blatantly disfigured portrayal of what the Mayan prophecies are said to convey by more authoritative sources. Playing on fear and purposeful distortion as a gimmick to stir people's sense of foreboding struck me as patently irresponsible. Nothing I have heard or seen since has changed my mind.

In the shower the next morning, my inner stirrings about this misrepresentation came quickly to the surface, with a clear inner understanding that I had a choice: I could complain or I could turn my feelings into some constructive good. At first, I shuddered at what I heard come to me: 'Yes, you can write another book and inform people with a more balanced viewpoint.' As an author already involved in writing two other books at the time—after just publishing twelve in about five years—that inner invitation met with mixed emotions: 'Oh, no, not another one; give me a break!' This was followed quickly by, 'I have no expertise at all in this field of endeavor—I'd have to find some experts willing to contribute chapters.' This reply rang through me: 'That's the idea; it will be much simpler and easier than it seems.' I responded with, 'Well, if it's so easy, what's the title?' '*2013!*' I laughed so hard that I almost slipped in the tub, and with that I knew the first step had been taken and there would be no turning back.

Later that week, I visited friends in Little Rock, and intuition prompted me at the dinner table to tell them about the shower incident. Marguerite told me that she was in a discussion group dealing with the book, *The Mystery of 2012*, and would be glad to lend me her copy. I took the book home and perused it for a sense of who I might ask to collaborate with me on putting a book together that would be akin to a primer—an entry-level book that would provide a wide enough range of perspectives to allow readers to make up their own mind about the potential for a different kind of 2012.

After searching the Internet for more information and other viewpoints, I initially invited a dozen experts from all ranges of perspectives to participate. In just a few days, not only had eight of the invitees responded affirmatively with enthusiasm, but one, Ervin Laszlo, pointed me to his organization, Wordshift 2012, and its co-initiator, Gareth Strangemore-Jones, who has also set up Worldshift Media as a new global multi-media conscious communications and event platform promoting the Worldshift Values of Peace, Justice, Sustainability, Social Innovation and Conscious Evolution (www.worldshift media.org). During our first conversation dealing with the potential for the book, Gareth offered to have their organization take responsibility for sending the book on its way. Then entered John Hunt, Publisher of O-Books, who volunteered to take this project on in collaboration with Worldshift 2012, a combination that is sure to make a huge contribution to bringing about greater social responsibility on this beloved planet of ours. John quickly saw the benefit of putting this volume on the fast track, making it available to readers far in advance of any normal publication time frame.

In just a few days, the book not only had begun to take form, but also had a firm commitment for publication and far-reaching distribution. It seemed like my 'inner guide' was absolutely correct—this was the easiest process I've ever encountered while publishing a book.

There's just one additional story to bring the tale of *2013!* full circle. Some friends invited me to join them on a trip to Merida, MX, in the Yucatan Peninsula—home to, no less, the Maya. As we finalized plans to go to Merida, I recalled some other friends of mine who conduct spiritually oriented tours into Maya country, and they connected me with Trudy Woodcock, of Casa K'in and Illuminado Tours, in Merida. Just as I was about to inquire about a tour, my phone rang; to my surprise and delight, it was Trudy. During our conversation, my intuition spoke up: 'Trudy, might you know any Mayas who would be both qualified and willing to write a chapter for a book on the Maya reality?'

'Oh, sure,' she responded instantaneously. 'Both Miguel and Eric—who work for our organization—they'd be eminently qualified. I don't know if they'd be willing, but I'll be glad to ask.'

A chill ran up my spine at the thought of Mayas lending additional authenticity to the delivery of information pertinent to the task at hand. We agreed that I would contact her to arrange a meeting to discuss this further when I arrived in Merida. True to my word, I immediately contacted Trudy and we decided to meet at Miguel's favorite restaurant for breakfast. I arrived a bit early, and when Miguel Angel Vergara walked into the restaurant a few minutes later our eyes met and I felt I had met a long lost brother. We embraced and immediately opened up to one another. Then Eric arrived, and the pattern repeated itself. Then Trudy, and once again the sense of Oneness appeared.

After explaining the intention of the book and why I thought their participation was so important, Trudy asked Miguel and Eric if they'd like to participate. Turning to them, she said she wanted to be sensitive to the fact that they may not feel fluent in English, so she volunteered to translate their works from Spanish. I could sense any hesitation on their part disappear in a cloud of relief. They both enthusiastically affirmed their desire to participate. Trudy turned to me and said, 'Jim, we are often asked to contribute articles and chapters, but this is the very first time we have accepted the invitation.' I was on cloud nine, to say the least. Since, Eric has had to respectfully decline, but Miguel's chapter lends Maya authenticity to the collection just the same.

There are other stories related to bringing this sterling cast of authors to one table, but I suspect that by now you have a sense that this collection was destined to be.

One admonition before you begin: I suggest that you focus on each chapter in ways that can assist in determining your own view. From time to time, go inward and see what your intuition is telling you about what you're reading—and discern what your feelings are telling you. You may want to ask yourself a few questions as you go along and at the end of each chapter. Something like these might inspire you: Does this make sense to me? Is the information accurate? Should I research the topic or information more to be sure that I understand? Is the information subject to different interpretation? How do I feel when I read this material? What do I feel inspired to do as a result of reading this chapter—and the entire collection? What is my view about 2012 now that I have all of these other perspectives in mind? How will my refined perspective influence how I live from day to day? I'm sure you have more questions and other intentions that can assist you in this inquiry. By all means, invest whatever you need in order to give yourself the result you want.

It is our collective hope that your heart and mind will be open in ways that will enable you to discern what resonates as Truth for you—and thus to demonstrate your Truth throughout each day. May the voice of inspiration be your guide.

Jim Young

Contributing Authors

Dr. Ervin Laszlo is the author or co-author of forty-seven books, translated into as many as twenty languages, and the editor of another thirty volumes, including a four-volume encyclopedia. He is Founder and President of The Club of Budapest; Founder and Director of the General Evolution Research Group; Chancellor-Nominee of the GlobalShift University; Fellow of the World Academy of Arts and Sciences; Member of the International Academy of Philosophy of Science; Senator of the International Medici Academy; and Editor of the international periodical World Futures: The Journal of General Evolution. Dr. Laszlo has a Ph.D. from the Sorbonne and is the recipient of four honorary Ph.D.s from the United States, Canada, Finland, and Hungary. He was awarded the Peace Prize of Japan, the Goi Award in Tokyo, 2002, and the International Mandir of Peace Prize in Assisi, 2005. He was nominated for the Nobel Peace Prize in 2004 and was re-nominated in 2005.

Dr. José A. Arguelles is the founder of Planet Art Network and the Foundation for the Law of Time, and holds a Ph.D. in art history and aesthetics from the University of Chicago. As one of the originators of the Earth Day concept, Arguelles founded the first Whole Earth Festival in 1970, and organized the Harmonic Convergence event of 1987. Now serving at the Galactic Institute, his book, *The Mayan Factor: Path Beyond Technology*, devises a numerological system that combines elements taken from the pre-Columbian Mayan Calendar, the I Ching, and other esoteric influences, interspersed with concepts drawn from modern sciences, such as 'genetic codes' and 'galactic convergences'. In his 2002 book, *Time and the Technosphere*, Arguelles devises and promotes what he calls the 'Law of Time', in part framed by his interpretations of how Mayan calendrical mathematics functioned. To Dr. Arguelles, 'the irregular 12-month [Gregorian] calendar and artificial, mechanized 60-minute hour' is a construct that artificially regulates human affairs, and is out-of-step with the natural 'synchronic order'.

Dr. Llewellyn Vaughn-Lee is a Sufi teacher and author. In recent years, the focus of his writing and teaching has been on spiritual responsibility in our present time of transition, and the emerging global consciousness of oneness: http://www.workingwithoneness.org. He has also specialized in the area of dream work, integrating the ancient Sufi approach to dreams with the insights of Jungian psychology. Llewellyn Vaughan-Lee is the founder of The Golden Sufi Center (www.goldensufi.org). His most recent books are: *The Return of the Feminine; The World Soul;* and *Alchemy of Light.*

Eden Sky has researched the revelatory time science of the Ancient Maya since 1995, and has studied directly under Dr. José Arguelles, who is largely responsible for the global interest in the Mayan Calendar System, and the now infamous 2012 date. As an Emissary of Galactic Culture, which affirms, 'Time is Art', she has produced an annual 13-Moon Natural Time Calendar for the past 15 years. A pioneering force within the worldwide movement focused on transforming humanity's relationship to the nature of time, Eden has participated in many international summits and conferences, and has been highly active in organizing community and educational gatherings that share the wisdom of Arguelles' solar-lunar-galactic calendar teachings. On a recent journey to Guatemala, Eden had the honor of partaking in ceremonies and teachings with Maya elders. Her passion is in sharing insights she has discovered on her path, that they might be pieces in others' cosmic puzzles.
www.13moon.com.

Geoff Stray is the author of *Beyond 2012: Catastrophe or Awakening, A Complete Guide to End-of-Time Predictions; The Mayan and Other Ancient Calendars;* and *2012 In Your Pocket—A Mini-Guide to the End of the World as You Know it.* His website is the web's most massive database on the subject: www.diagnosis2012.co.uk. Geoff gives presentations in Europe and the USA and has appeared in documentaries, such as *2012: The Odyssey; Transformation 2013;* and *2012: An Awakening.* His chapter began as an essay, first appearing in *New Dawn Magazine* Nov/Dec 2009: www.newdawnmagazine.com.

Dr. Mark Van Stone has studied and practiced the calligraphy and carving of all cultures since childhood. He spent 1972 studying Celtic Manuscript Illumination in the libraries of Ireland and Britain. In 1982-83 he apprenticed as a netsuke carver in Japan with Sensei Saito Bishu, the first foreigner ever to do so. In 1988 he received a Guggenheim Fellowship to study and photograph ancient writing around the world. In 1990 he worked for Will Vinton Studios, learning Claymation®, sculpting California Raisins®. In 1994, he began studying formally under Linda Schele at the University of Texas, earning his M.A. in 1996, and his Ph.D. in 2005. Along the way, he illustrated and co-authored *Reading the Maya Glyphs* with Michael Coe in 2001. In 2003 and 2005, he presented papers comparing Egyptian and Maya writing systems, and on the origins of the Alphabet, at the *Writing Systems of the World* Conference at the Alexandria Library in Egypt. Presently Professor of Art History at Southwestern College in Chula Vista, California, he has just completed a new book of essays, *2012: Science and Prophecy of the Ancient Maya.*

Dr. Carl Johan Calleman has a Ph.D. in Physical Biology from the University of Stockholm. He has been a Senior Researcher at the University of Washington in Seattle, and a cancer expert for the WHO. He is the author of *The Purposeful Universe* (Inner Traditions, 2009), a book that presents a new theory of biological evolution based on the Cosmic Tree of Life. He currently teaches at the online International Metaphysical University (http://www. intermetu.com/). He held his first talk with the mention of the end of the Mayan calendar in 1979 and is the only professional scientist to have studied the *meaning* of the Mayan calendar (many professional Mayanists have studied the calendar as such, but not its reality basis in biological and historical evolution). He has authored: *Solving the Greatest Mystery of Our Time: The Mayan Calendar* (Garev, 2001) and *The Mayan calendar and the Transformation of Consciousness* (Inner Traditions, 2004). His website is www.calleman.com, and he is also associated with the websites: www.mayanmajix.com, http://mayaportal.lucita.net and www.shiftoftheages.com.

Gill Edwards is a clinical psychologist in England who has been involved in mind-body medicine for thirty years. She is trained in shamanism, energy psychology and energy medicine, and is the author of *Living Magically; Life is a Gift; Wild Love,* and other books. Following a diagnosis of breast cancer, she committed herself to a healing journey of conscious evolution—and discovered that the cancer had truly been a remarkable gift. Her latest book, *Conscious Medicine,* will be published by Piatkus in November, 2010. www.livingmagically.co.uk

Miguel Angel Vergara is a Mayan Priest and Master Teacher who lives and works in Yucatán, Mexico. He studied with Mayan Elder Don Vincente Martín for seventeen years in the Yucatán, was a director at Chichen Itzá for four years, and has given lectures and workshops throughout North America and Europe. He teaches us how to connect with the Masters of Light, who are still here at the sacred Maya sites, ready to guide us now as in ancient times. He goes to the source of the Maya knowledge:

to the ceremonies, rituals, mantras, sacred books, pyramids, temples, stele, pottery, paintings, sculptures, and oral traditions that are available today to find the essence of their knowledge, and then teaches in a heart-centered style that connects rapidly and profoundly with his students. Miguel Angel's mission is to share the sacred Maya teachings through the study of their science, art, philosophy, and religion. He currently leads spiritual tours throughout the Maya world of Yucatán, Chiapas, and Guatemala. Miguel Angel also conducts workshops, seminars, lectures, and classes on the Ancient Maya Wisdom in Mexico, USA, Canada and Europe: info@casakin.org.

Martien and Teressena Bakens have facilitated sacred group journeys to Mayan and Olmec sites in Mexico and Guatemala, working with shamans and elders in these areas. They have been invited to become part of the new cosmic University in Merida, founded by mentor and Mayan teacher, Don Miguel Angel Vergara.

Teressena Bakens, the creator and illustrator of *The Fifth Tarot*, is a visionary artist and intuitive. Her drawings help awaken one's inner knowing and wisdom of the sacred. Teressena works as a spiritual midwife, helping people heal and transform through shamanic ceremony. She also facilitates workshops on the Goddess and the divine feminine. She is the author of *Peace Moon* and is currently working on her new book, *Teachings of the Serpent*.

Martien Bakens, author of *The Fifth Tarot*, is an energy healer, aroma therapist and alchemist. He received his formal training in Europe in various holistic healing modalities in both Eastern and Western traditions. His intuitive writings offer profound insights into the spiritual laws of the universe, creating a greater understanding of our multi-dimensional gifts and possibilities. www.thefifthtarot.com and www.peacevalleycreations.com

Dr. Jim Young has served with distinction as a teacher and distinguished professor of higher education, and in a variety of leadership positions, including President of State University of New York at Potsdam and Chancellor of the University of Arkansas at Little Rock. He is an award winning spiritual author, poet and photographer, applying the reframing of spiritual perspective in all aspects of his life's calling. His photographs are regularly juried into national and international art and photography exhibitions and are found in collections around the world. A ministerial graduate of the Pecos Benedictine Monastery's ecumenical school for spiritual directors and the Minister Emeritus for the Creative Life Church in Hot Springs, AR, Jim was also a co-founder and facilitator for the AR Metaphysical Society in Eureka Springs and The Aristotle Group in Hot Springs, AR. Author of a vast array of spiritual books, new in 2010 are: *Aware in a World Asleep* and *God's pocket Dictionary*. Dr. Young is an inspirational teacher who takes participants to the threshold of their own Truth. He is available for workshops, seminars and presentations. Website: www. creationspirit.net. To make arrangements: 1Andrea.Thomas@gmail.com.

Nicolya Christi is an author, global activist, global futurist and consciousness evolutionist. She is a leading campaigner, catalyst and actionist in the evolution of consciousness. Nicolya is the founder of the Worldshift Movement (www.worldshift-movement.org) and is a core member of the WorldShift 2012 Executive Committee. Her primary purpose is to promote and support the process of an 'Inner-World Shift', as a prerequisite to attaining a lasting 'World Shift'. Nicolya is a spiritual teacher, soul mentor, workshop facilitator and therapist, who holds a B.A. in Metaphysical Sciences and is trained in Psycho-Synthesis Psychotherapy. www.nicolyachristi.com.

Aluna Joy Yaxk'in is an internationally renowned author, spiritual life coach, sacred site guide, alternative historian, ordained minister and modern mystic who inspires and encourages others to recognize and accept their own authentic divinity and connection to God. www.AlunaJoy.com

Just when the caterpillar thought its world was over—
it became a butterfly.
Anonymous

Chapter One

Chaos Point 2012: Science and Prophecy

Dr. Ervin Laszlo

There is a growing wave of thinking that associates the coming of a chaos point with the famous end of 2012 date. Some people contest this assumption and go as far as to claim that all talk of a chaos point is mistaken; the world as it is today will not change, at least not in our lifetime. Others take the contrary view; they claim that it's already too late: the chaos point has already been passed. This is the view expressed by, among others, James Lovelock, the British scientist who, thirty years ago, worked out how the Earth possesses a planetary-scale control system that keeps it fit for life (the 'Gaia hypothesis').

Lovelock maintains that the 'Gaia system' is out of control. 'I think we have little option,' he wrote in *The Revenge of Gaia* (February, 2006), 'but to prepare for the worst, and assume that we have passed the threshold. The Earth's physical condition must be seen as seriously ill and soon to pass into a morbid fever that may last as long as 100,000 years.' The principal reason for this pessimistic assessment is global warming. The heating up of the atmosphere will create 'a hell of a climate.' The average temperature will rise 8 degrees centigrade in temperate regions and 5 degrees in the tropics.

Is Lovelock right—have we reached a catastrophic chaos point already? When we take a closer look at his argument, we find room for a more positive assessment. Lovelock's reasoning about the dynamics of the Earth's physical-biological systems is sound, but he doesn't recognize that not only nature, but also humanity, is a dynamic system on the threshold of a chaos point.

Human societies, the same as the planetary ecologies, are not infinitely stressable. Sooner or later they reach the point where they tip one way or another. When that chaos point is reached, they become ultra-sensitive and capable of rapid transformation. The dangers, as well as the opportunities conveyed by chaos points, apply to natural as well as to human systems.

Will the coming of a chaos point in human societies coincide with the famous 2012 prophecies? Many people say so, but such claims need to be substantiated. For the most part, the claims refer to esoteric prophecies coming from traditional cultures. These may convey important information and merit being known. But is there scientific evidence to back them up?

The Prophecies

The most famous of the prophecies that speak of the end of 2012 as a critical point in human life and civilization is undoubtedly that of the Mayans. The Mayans viewed civilization as a cyclic process, where shifts from one phase of the cycle to the next occur at measurable intervals.

The cyclic concept of the world was not unique to the Mayans. Cycles exist everywhere in nature and have been recognized in almost all cultures. In the biosphere some cycles are daily, others seasonal or annual. Roughly twenty-four-hour circadian cycles govern many of our bodily functions in accordance with the alternation of day and night. Menstrual cycles average twenty-eight days, and the ebb and flow of tidal waters reflect the changing positions of the Moon and Sun relative to the Earth. Solar cycles displayed by the frequency of sunspots last about eleven years, with the solar maximum and solar minimum recurring in each cycle.

Cycles have been perceived in history as well. In traditional cultures, they were seen as the advent and passing of 'Great Ages'. These include the astrological Great Year, which lasts just under twenty-six thousand years (based on the precession of the equinoxes), as well as the Yugas of Hindu philosophy, a cosmic epoch with a cycle of dark and golden ages: the Kaly yuga (Iron Age), the Dwapara yuga (Bronze Age), Treta yuga (Silver Age), and Satya yuga (Golden Age). Many myths speak of celestial cycles, and many civilizations have attempted to map their principal transitions. Celestial calendars were a major reference for life in many parts of the world. One of the most famous of these calendars is the Tzolk'in calendar, a 260-day Mesoamerican system that was known to the Mayans.

Modern historians, among them Arnold Toynbee and Pitirim Sorokin, had also advanced a cyclic interpretation of history. Toynbee viewed civilization as a movement rather than a condition, exhibiting a 'life cycle' where eight years is the period of gestation, eighty the period of physical self-expression, and 800 the total life-span.

The Mayan's interpretation of history is embedded in their calendar, completed by priest-astronomers in the year 1479 and carved into the Aztec-Mayan sunstone. The Mayan calendar details long passages of time, including mathematical calculations so accurate that modern astronomers are at a loss to understand how a traditional people could arrive at them (for example, the calculation of the length of the Earth's revolution within a thousandth of a decimal point).

The most famous calculation is encoded in the so-called long count. The 'Age of Jaguar', the thirteenth *baktun* of 144,000 days, will come to an end on the 21st of December 2012. That will mark the end of the Fourth Sun (also known as the Fourth World) and the end—and at the same time also the beginning— of the Mayan calendar. This transformative date is written as 13.0.0.0.0 in long count notation, which is the same as the notation for the first day in the calendar.

December 21, 2012 marks the end of the long count in the Mayan calendar (and thus also the end and rebirth of the calendar), but not the end of the world. Carlos Barrios, a

Guatemalan historian and anthropologist who became a Mayan Ajq'ij ceremonial priest and spiritual guide, is currently the most authentic spokesperson for the Mayan elders. He is definite on the question regarding the end of the world.

Other people write about prophecy in the name of the Maya, They say that the world will end on December 2012. The Mayan elders are angry with this. The world will not end. It will be transformed.

Everything will change: December 21, 2012 will be a date of rebirth, the beginning of the World of the Fifth Sun. The nature of that world is not determined in advance, but the Mayan system suggests that it may be the beginning of a new cycle of Ages, starting with the Golden Age. It is likely to mark a fundamental shift in human culture and consciousness.

A world transformation at the end of 2012 is predicted by astrology as well. Astrologers have noted that at sunrise on December 21, 2012 the Sun will conjunct the intersection of the Milky Way and the plane of the ecliptic, creating a cosmic cross. The center of our galaxy will complete a 'cosmic year', a 25,920-year journey around the wheel of the zodiac. According to most systems of astrology, a new cosmic year will then begin, lasting for another 25,920 years. (The reality of this cycle—if not its astrological or Mayan interpretation—rests on independent scientific evidence: it concerns the rotation of the Earth on its axis. This rotation is about 23 degrees off vertical: our planet is like a spinning top that is slightly out of balance. In this condition it takes 25,800 years for the celestial pole to describe a full circle. The conjunction noted by Mayans and astrologers will occur in a 36-year window in time between 1980 and 2016. The Mayans have chosen the winter solstice 2012 as the decisive point, even though it's not in the middle of this window, perhaps because at that point the Earth's axis will point exactly toward the 'galactic bulge'—the thick central part of the visual image of the Milky Way galaxy as seen from Earth.)

The cosmic conjunction noted by both astrologers and Mayans is seen as a fundamental realignment in a number of other spiritual traditions, including the Hopi time-keeping system, Vedic and Islamic astrology, Mithraism, the Jewish kabala, European sacred geography, medieval Christian architecture, and a variety of hermetic metaphysics.

Mystical philosopher Terence McKenna arrived at the 2012 date on the basis of mathematical calculations based on the *I Ching*. McKenna's 'timewave' takes account of the ebb and flow of novelty in the universe. The great periods of novelty began about four billion years ago when the planet was formed, and continued sixty-five million years before our time, when the dinosaurs became extinct and mammals diffused over the continents. There was a surge of novelty between 15,000 and 8,000 B.C.E., the approximate period of the Neolithic Revolution and the birth of agriculture with settled communities. Another surge occurred around 500 B.C.E., when Lao-Tzu, Plato, Zoroaster, Buddha, and other seminal figures appeared on the stage of history. The calculation yields further novelty waves in the late eighteenth century, at the epoch of social and scientific revolutions, in the turbulent 1960s, and in the early twenty-first century, coinciding with the time of the 9/11 terrorist attack. The next peak of novelty fell on November of 2008, which was the date of the transformative U.S. elections, and another wave is to occur in October of 2010. The waves are to culminate on the 21st of December 2012. At that point, novelty is to reach infinity — anything and everything conceivable to the mind could then occur at the same time.

The Evidence

What independent evidence do we have that the 2012 prophecies harbor an element of truth? Are there scientifically established grounds to believe not only that an interesting conjunction will occur in the position of our planet at the end of 2012, but that this conjunction will signify a tipping point for all of humanity?

First of all, we should review what is meant by a tipping point, from the independent and impartial perspective of science. The disciplines known collectively as the systems sciences (general systems and general evolution theory, chaos theory, cybernetics, information and complexity theory, and non-equilibrium thermodynamics, among others) describe a tipping point as a state of chaos in a system. At that point, so-called 'chaotic' or 'strange' attractors replace more stable point or periodic attractors in the 'phase portrait' of the system, and the new attractors induce chaotic conditions in that system. This is not a purely random, aleatory condition, but a highly ordered one. It produces complex, finely tuned behavior that departs from the previously established behavior of the system. The system's behavior becomes complex and highly sensitive to perturbation. In such a condition even small changes—whether they occur in the system's environment, or within the system— produce major effects: the so-called 'butterfly' effects. In a condition of chaos the system is prone to sudden change and profound transformation.

There is evidence that the systems of life on this planet approach such a chaos-based tipping point. The evidence comes both from nature, and from our own human systems. Weather patterns turn extreme over the whole world; the changes range from droughts in China and Australia, floods in North America and increased cyclone activity, to devastating hurricanes that impact tropical coastlines and move inland. Threats to health surface on a scale never before experienced: avian flu and 'novel swine flu', malaria and other tropical diseases believed to have been vanquished. Global warming creates a widespread and frequent incidence of vector-borne diseases such as malaria and dengue fever, as well as of water-borne diseases such as cholera.

Climate change is a major factor of stress in the contemporary world, but not the only factor. The record shows global and local temperatures strongly fluctuating. The average is rising: in the summer of 2003 temperature fluctuations averaged 2.3 degrees higher than in previous years. Globally, temperatures have risen over the past century by at least 0.74°C, and the principal causes are still debated. More than likely, both human and natural processes conspire to produce the warming. It is known that greenhouse gases in the Earth's atmosphere trap the sun's rays and heat up the atmosphere. This is bound to be a factor in global warming, whether or not changes in the physical processes of the Sun contribute to the warming.

Global warming is also produced by natural causes. As well as the emission of CO_2 and other greenhouses gases, variations in the sun's radiation and in sunspot activity, variations in the Earth's orbit and spin, and volcanic geo-thermal activity affect and warm the planet's troposphere and stratosphere.

In its 2007 Report, the Intergovernmental Panel on Climate Change (IPCC) declared that the warming of the world's climate is now 'unequivocal'. This is a matter of observed fact. It comes to the fore in the increase of temperatures in the arctic, in the reduced size of icebergs and the melting of icecaps and glaciers, in the reduction of areas under permafrost, in changes in rainfall patterns, and in new wind formations, droughts, heat waves, tropical cyclones, and other extreme weather patterns.

The consequences of global warming include widespread flooding due to tropical storms and the rise of sea levels. The melting of the Greenland icecap could alter the flow of the Gulf Stream and may deflect it before it reaches the European continent, dropping temperatures in England and the Nordic countries to levels typical of Labrador. If the West Antarctic ice sheet disintegrates, during this century the level of the sea would rise by meters and not centimeters and human settlements close to sea level would be inundated.

According to the Stern Review, commissioned by the British government in 2007, there is a 50 percent risk of global temperatures rising by more than a 5°C by the year 2100. In a conservative formulation, this would create a '5 to 20 percent reduction in consumption levels' worldwide. But even a global temperature increase of 3°C would radically transform the flows and balances of the ecology on which animal, plant and human life is now vitally dependent.

Global stress is further induced by the growth of the world's population. At the end of the twentieth century population was growing by about 900 million per decade, equivalent to a new London every month. It passed 6 billion before the turn of the century, and demographic calculations indicate that it would reach 9.1 billion by the middle of the 21st century. Urban dwellers number more than half of the world's population, and U.N. forecasts speak of 60 percent of the global population living in cities by 2030.

Modern cities are the largest conglomerations of humans ever seen on this planet. There are mega-conglomerations such as the Greater Tokyo Area with 35 million inhabitants, and Sao Paolo with 23 or 25 million. Other cities are rapidly catching up: Mumbai, Delhi, Mexico City, Dhaka, Jakarta and Lagos, among others. By 2015, there may be 23 mega-cities in the world, 19 of them in the developing world, and 37 cities with populations between 5 and 10 million.

Rapid urbanization in developing countries exposes vast numbers of poor people to shortages of drinking water and sanitation, as well as to rising air pollution and air-born toxins. Large cities produce enormous social inequalities; over one billion people now squat in squalor in slums, favelas and bidonvilles.

Urban overcrowding and sub-minimal conditions of life in urban conglomerations are major factors that stress people in many parts of the world. They produce frustration and conflict, resulting in higher levels of violence and unusual forms of crime: mass murders, when seemingly ordinary people run amok, renewed suicide bombing in populated city centers, and suicidal terrorism on land and in the air.

The rapid growth of the world's population, especially the growth of cities, creates growing problems of energy. Urban centers consume three-quarters of the world's energy and are responsible for at least three-quarters of its pollution. The supply of abundant cheap energy has entered a critical end-phase. As the world continues to run on fossil fuels, demand for oil rises and supply diminishes. At the beginning of the second decade of the twenty-first century, most of the world's oil-producers had passed their peak. The largest oilfields were discovered over half a century ago: the peak of discovery was in 1965. New fields have not been found at the same rate, and as a result global oil production will peak, or has already peaked. As the peak is passed, oil becomes more difficult and expensive to extract. The supply of cheap oil drops, and extraction becomes less profitable. Yet demand for oil is still rising: the International Energy Agency found that in the last few years, global demand has been increasing by 2 million barrels a day. If no significant changes in the patterns of energy production and consumption come about, global demand for oil would rise in the next two decades, from the present 80 million barrels a day to 125 million barrels.

Growing demand and decreasing supply drive prices up. Surges in oil prices impact almost instantly on people, enter-prises and economies in every part of the world. Higher prices also trigger conflict related to discovery and extraction. The Arctic Ocean seabed, which may hold billions of gallons of both oil and natural gas, is becoming a globally contested region. In March 2007, Russia made public that it plans to set up a military force to protect its interests in the Arctic, and in August of that year the Russian flag had been planted on the ocean bed 4 km beneath the North Pole to indicate Russia's claim to the undersea oil-formation known as the Lomonosov Ridge. The

U.K. in turn is claiming sovereign rights over more than 1 million square kilometers (386,000 square miles) of the seabed off Antarctica. The opening up of the Northwest Passage due to the melting of Arctic ice is already provoking international contestation and conflict.

Physical changes in the intensity of solar radiation conspire with anthropic impacts to create stress in the system. Astronomers have noted that since the 1940s, and particularly since 2003, the Sun has become remarkably turbulent. Solar activity is predicted to peak around 2012, creating storms of intensity unprecedented since the 1859 'Carrington event', when a large solar flare, accompanied by a coronal mass ejection, flung billions of tons of solar plasma into the Earth's magnetosphere.

Solar storms, capable of traveling at speeds up to 5 million miles per hour, could knock-out virtually every major technological infrastructure on the planet: transportation, security and emergency response systems, electricity grids, finance, telecommunications, including satellite and other wireless networks, and even household electronic equipment. The solar storm of 1859 was the most powerful event of its kind in recorded history. On the 1st of September of that year the Sun expelled huge quantities of high-energy protons in a large flare that traveled directly toward the Earth, taking eighteen hours instead of the usual three or four days to reach our planet. It disrupted telegraph systems all over Europe and North America. Fires erupted in telegraph stations due to power surges in the wires; and the northern lights (aurora borealis) were seen as far south as Florida.

The next solar storm on record, in March of 1989, melted the transformers of the Hydro-Quebec Power Grid, causing a nine-hour blackout that affected six million people in Canada. And the solar storms that reached the Earth between October 19th and November 7th 2003 disrupted satellites and global communications, air travel, navigation systems, and power grids all over the world. It also affected systems on the International Space Station.

The solar maximum forecast for 2012 would do greater harm than any before, since human life has become more dependent on the global energy grid. According to 'Severe Space Weather Events: Understanding Economic and Societal Impacts', a National Research Council report issued in the spring of 2009 by the U.S. National Academy of Sciences, another Carrington event would induce ground currents that would knock out 300 key transformers within 90 seconds and cut off power for more than 130 million people in the U.S. alone. Its cost could be as high as 2 trillion dollars, and recovery time would be four to ten years. An even worse impact would be felt in China, where the electrical grid is more vulnerable than in the West.

A major solar storm would cause the failure of electric power in most parts of the world. The above-cited report of the National Academy of Science claims that this would have catastrophic consequences. People in high-rise apartments, where water has to be pumped up, would be cut off immediately. For most others, drinking water would come through the taps for about half a day, but the flow would then cease without electricity to pump it from reservoirs. Transportation systems directly or indirectly dependent on electric power (which means practically all systems) would come to a standstill. Back-up generators would operate at some sites until their fuel ran out. For hospitals, that would mean about 72 hours of essential care only services. Without power for heating, cooling and refrigeration, and with a breakdown in the distribution of medicines and pharmaceuticals, urban population could begin to die back within days.

Scientists forecast yet another disruptive event for the end of 2012: breaches in the Earth's magnetic field. In the past, this field protected living systems from the effects of solar storms and coronal mass ejections. Lately, the magnetic field has diminished in intensity and holes and gaps have appeared. Scientists in South Africa measured cracks in the magnetic field the size of California. In December of 2008, NASA announced that its Themis Project had found a massive breach that would allow a devastating amount of solar plasma to enter the Earth's magnetosphere.

The fluctuation of the magnetic field could also lead to the reversal of the planet's magnetic poles. During the course of reversal, the magnetic field would become still weaker, and the danger to life from solar and stellar radiation would greatly increase.

Another scientific report of relevance concerns the entry of our solar system into a highly energized region of space. This turbulent region is making the Sun hotter and stormier and has already caused climate change on other planets. According to Russian scientists, the effects on Earth will include an acceleration of the magnetic pole shift, the vertical and horizontal distribution of ozone, and an increase in the frequency and magnitude of extreme climate events.

Quite apart from mystical and esoteric prophecies, there is solid evidence that 2012 will be a turbulent period. Will we be ready for it—ready to cope with the shifts and disruptions, and to seize the opportunities that come in their wake? This is the question responsible people, enterprises and governments now need to confront. It is the question to which I, as well as the Club of Budapest and the mission-oriented WorldShift 2012 programs I have initiated, are dedicated.

Chapter Two

The 2012 Prophecy and the Harmonic Convergence of 2012

Dr. José A. Arguelles

2012. It seems that date is increasingly on everybody's mind. The release of the Roland Emmerich film, *2012*, on November 12, 2009, has popularized this date on a planetary scale. What does it mean? Where did it come from? As awareness of that date becomes an event of mass consciousness, we begin to sense the coming of something of the greatest magnitude, a veritable world shift. Its ripples are creating the first waves, washing up on the shores of the old consciousness. What is behind December 21, 2012 that it would create such an effect?

It is generally known that this date is related to the Mayan calendar and the Mayan prophecies. How did the Maya come to this date, and what do their prophecies say about it?

The Maya, whose civilization reached its heights in Central America and Mexico between AD 435 and 830, were expert mathematicians with a unique and superb calendar. They used many calendars—at least seventeen simultaneously—and had a mathematical system that staggers the imagination. Yet, by materialist anthropological standards, they were culturally a late stone-age people! If this is to be believed, who were they and how did they come to be operating with a sophisticated sense of time far beyond anything known even today?

In contemplating these facts, and through profound meditation and a life-long study of the mathematical system of the Maya, I have concluded that such an advanced achievement could only be a reflection of an advanced civilization and system of knowledge whose origins are beyond Maya, and were operating with a galactic time science. (See: *The Mayan Factor, Path beyond Technology,* 1987.)

According to the time-science of the ancient Maya, our history has been shaped by a galactic beam, and a great moment of transformation awaits us at 2012, when we pass out of that beam. The primary intention of the Mayan calendar system was not to measure time but to record the harmonic calibrations of this synchronization beam, 5,125-years or 5200-tun (360-day cycles) in duration.

December 21, 2012 marks the precise conclusion of the passage of our solar system through this galactic synchronization beam. For humanity, this beam constitutes the *wave harmonic of history.* Why? The beam, 5,125 years in diameter, commenced 13 August B.C. 3113, a date marked by the Mayan calendar long count as 13.0.0.0.0, 4 Ahau. This precise date 13.0.0.0.0, 4 Ahau will occur again on December 21, 2012. Exactly 1,872,000 days will have passed, a cycle of 13 *baktuns* of 144,000 days each. This interval, B.C. 3113 – A.D. 2012, comprises the totality of history as we know it—from the First Dynasty of Egypt to the Twin Towers—hence *wave harmonic of history.*

During this cycle, humanity has gone from a tribal creature just learning how to live in cities, to being a full-blown planetary organism. The conclusion of the cycle in A.D. 2012—kin 1,872,000, 13.0.0.0.0—bodes nothing less than a major evolutionary upgrading of the planetary life process. At this point, a resonant frequency phase shift will occur, ushering us into the brilliance of the post-2012 era of our galactic-solar-planetary evolution. We shall understand that we have passed not only into a post-historic but post-human, or super human, phase of our evolution.

If we speak of a 'galactic synchronization beam'; what is this beam and what is it synchronizing? We are dealing with an intelligently focused, high frequency *time beam* that is calibrated by thirteen sub-cycles called baktuns. Each sub-cycle is approximately 394.5 solar years or 144,000 days in duration. Each baktun is further divided into 20 smaller cycles called katuns, 260 in all. Each baktun was holographically charged with a program for activating and synchronizing the collective human DNA and its mental capacity into slow but steady increments of expansion and acceleration—process characterized by military conquest, imperialist colonization and consumption of material resources.

During the twelfth baktun, A.D. 1224-1618, all of the major civilizations reached an apex of expansion and pre-industrial complexity, spilling over from the Old World to the New with the European Conquest of the Americas and circumnavigation of the Earth. This set the stage for the thirteenth and final baktun, A.D.1618-2012.

During this concluding baktun, the cumulative effects of the first twelve cycles attained an exponential momentum, known as the 'climax of matter'. Not only does the year 1618 inaugurate what is usually referred to as the 'scientific revolution', but it also marks the beginning of the mechanization of time and consciousness. This fact, more than any other, sets the final baktun apart from all of the previous ones. For the mechanization of time, through the perfection of the mechanical clock, creates an alienation from nature, and a highly advanced capacity for social complexification and technological acceleration unlike anything hitherto known.

The process of the mechanization of time also created a totally unconscious mental field in which the human systematically separated itself from nature for the purpose of creating a vast industrialized order eventually to be known as the technosphere—a sphere or bubble of artificial time cast over the biosphere. Henceforth, the human species was to be living on its own artificial time, apart from the rest of the biosphere that continues to operate in the natural cycles.

Artificial time was to be a double-edged sword. On the one hand, immersion in artificial time allowed the human species to construct a fantastically elaborate and complicated global civilization. On the other hand, in separating itself from the natural cycles of universal order, a profoundly materialistic belief system was created that has crippled the biosphere in its pursuit of resources and profits, while fomenting a psychology of alienation that has resulted in today's global mega crisis.

In the thirteen-baktun context, the human race is viewed as a single planetary organism. In entering the artificial time of the thirteenth baktun, the human DNA became an excited and agitated field, extruding technology much like a spider extrudes its web. The purpose of technology and the pursuit of materialism allow the previously dispersed human community to come together, however chaotically, to finally realize itself as a single life form capable of existing anywhere in the biosphere. This end result is the cumulative effect of the 5,125-year synchronization beam.

The process of arriving at this globalized condition has occurred so rapidly that the human mind, with its various provincial values shaped by antagonistic tribal, religious and nationalistic beliefs, has hardly had a chance to rise up from the conflict it has engendered to see that we are in actuality a single planetary organism.

Despite the present day crisis, 'Little do the humans realize how close they are to the moment when the genetic game board of their reality becomes the illumined design of galactic destiny' (*Mayan Factor*, p.154.)

Other factors to consider in reviewing the significance and meaning of 2012 include: first, the intensity of interest in the 2012 date is itself a manifestation of the process of acceleration and synchronization engendered by the galactic beam. Until the *Mayan Factor* was published in 1987, when the 2012 date was first dropped into the mass consciousness, next to no one knew about it. The purpose of the *Mayan Factor* was to alert people to the conclusion of the cycle of history in 2012, and the tremendous shift in consciousness this date augured. In the ensuing years, curiosity about the date developed slowly. However, since 2007, interest in 2012 has become a feature of the mass consciousness, inclusive of books, websites, documentaries and feature length Hollywood films. To many people it is the end of time, the end of the Mayan calendar, even the apocalypse, as witnessed by the recently released Roland Emmerich film, *2012*, with its dark intensity and publicity caption that reads 'we were warned'.

These are popular misperceptions that unfortunately get raised to the status of supernatural reality by the entertainment industry. But the mass interest, whether fearful or hopeful, is already a shift in consciousness. Something is going to happen. But what that is actually is up to us. We can go into fear or we can generate the kind of positive co-creative script the world needs in order to conclude and regenerate the cycle on a successful evolutionary note.

Second, there is the advent of the *noosphere*. The galactic synchronization, foreseen as the conclusion of the cycle in 2012, is the moment of an evolutionary shift or mutation. In fact, the entire 5,125-year cycle—but an instant of geological time—could be seen as a mutative phase. This phase complete, a new evolutionary stage begins. This is known as the *noosphere*—literally, the mental sheathe of the planet, the mind of the Earth—where we think and act as one planetary organism.

In fact, what we refer to as the crises are but the various effects of the *biosphere-noosphere transition*, the chaotic and dissipative shift into the new order of planetary reality. As a planetary organism, we are now being inevitably pushed into a new condition of *planetary consciousness*, the noosphere.

This process, already underway, is an aspect of our evolutionary mutation. As a critical mass develops, it will snowball into a consciousness shift, the most primary prerequisite for entering the noosphere and creating the peaceable world envisioned for the decades following 2012.

Ervin Laszlo defines the coming consciousness event as 'Worldshift 2012', and in his book of the same title he makes this the principle point: 'Preparing for an effective Worldshift by the end of 2012 is now the top planetary priority.' Such a quantum shift achieved through evolution of our consciousness *is* the program of the noosphere, as well as the galactic significance of 2012.

As *Worldshift 2012* points out, there is a path to 2012. It is not a matter of passively waiting for something to happen. Once one has heard about 2012, one is called to action to help define the new reality. To make this a coherent process, a virtual 'Noosphere Forum' has been called into being (www.noosphere-forum.org). Its first stage is activation through the cybersphere and the convening of bioregional noosphere congresses. We are now in the second stage and that is expanding the network of a 'noosphere collective' — a compilation and cross-fertilization of all kindred groups and organizations, as well as establishing an expanded curriculum, 'Science and Theory of the Rainbow Bridge'. The end result of the cumulative positive activity will be the Harmonic Convergence of 2012.

Which brings us to the third point concerning 2012: the perception of time. According to the Mayan view, time is a frequency (13:20), the universal factor of synchronization. In this light, the universe is an ever-evolving harmony giving rise to the value: *time is art*. As the frequency shift occurs, the old calendar will be replaced by a new one based on the harmonic standard of thirteen moons/28 days, and rooted in the 13:20 frequency. This new calendar is already used in many parts of the world (see www.lawoftime.org). By this means, the philosophy of *time is money* gives way to the new value of *time is art*. This fundamental shift will give rise to a new collective human priority: instead of ransacking the Earth for resources, we shall seek to transform the Earth into a work of art. This perception will be of inestimable value in shifting our post-2012 priorities.

Finally, considering that Earth is a member of the heliosphere—the solar system as a living organism—2012 augurs a new solar age, what is referred to in the Mexican prophecies as 'the coming sixth sun of consciousness'. Exploring the relation between solar frequencies and our own psychic powers, which the Maya term *tinkinantah*, the more adventurous members of our race will evolve a science of bio-solar telepathy, establishing a sure means for our continuing evolution. By creating a planetary telepathic network, the notion that the noosphere is the mental sheathe of the planet will be realized. The cosmic consciousness of the noosphere will be the supreme legacy of our 2012 mind shift, the awakening of the Harmonic Convergence of 2012.

The best is yet to come.

Chapter Three

A Prophecy and a Prayer

Llewellyn Vaughn-Lee, Ph.D.

I.
Time and the Moment

Are we facing a global catastrophe or a golden age, or both? As 2012 comes closer with its Mayan prophecies of the end of time, we are being forced to face the realities of an ecological disaster on a global level. There are also signs of a shift in consciousness away from a culture steeped in materialism towards values that reflect a more holistic understanding of life. The year 2012 has been given to us as a watershed, the moment in which our civilization could either collapse or transform. What does this mean, and what does this mean to us now, in this present moment of time?

First, one needs to acknowledge that, from a spiritual perspective, only the moment of now exists. One of the most basic spiritual teachings is that time itself is an illusion, and only the present moment is real. Spiritual awakening, when we step out of our self-created illusion to experience the world and our self in its true, divine nature, only happens in the present moment, not as some plan for the future or memory of the past. This is the Zen moment of *satori*, when we taste the sweetness of the fruit for the first time, and it is *always* for the first time. There is no time, but just the moment that *is*, and in this moment everything is present according to its true nature. This is the dimension of the Self, the *atman*, to which we are given access. And in the Self there is no time, just the continually unfolding, ever-changing and yet unchanging present.

So, if one understands or has experienced this spiritual truth, what concern can one have about a specific time in the future? If only the moment of now exists, then the future is as much an illusion as the past, and why should a spiritually awake individual be concerned with an illusion? The simplest answer is that the majority of humanity is living in a dream, as Shakespeare reminds us: 'We are such stuff as dreams are made on'. And in this dream past and future *do* exist. However insubstantial, this dream matters for those who live within it. It is the substance of their daily life, their hopes and fears, their joys and tears. And although it is easy to say that it is all an illusion, one remembers the story of the Zen student who, when he said this to his teacher, was hit hard by the teacher's stick, and when he shouted in pain, was asked by the teacher, 'Was that an illusion?'

In this unfolding dream that we call life, a crisis is coming. We are destroying our own ecosystem, and we are beginning to realize that this system is reaching a breaking point, a point where it cannot be repaired, cannot return to its previous state of balance. And we have no understanding, no past knowledge or experience, of what this might mean. What could happen if the ecological imbalance of the world began to spiral out of control? Some would argue that time is running out, but that we still have a few years to make the necessary changes and stabilize the situation. Other people might say that moment has passed, that the clock has already struck twelve, and environmental changes are accelerating uncontrollably—we just do not yet realize this, are blinded by our belief in science and materialism, by our false hopes and fears.

Only the moment is real, and yet we live in a world that is rushing towards a future with global forces spinning out of control. These two paradoxical truths can be held together, must be held together, if we are to bring balance back into our lives and the life of the planet. To take full responsibility for our

35

present predicament means to be present and awake, because only in the moment can we make a real contribution. Only in the moment can we effect the changes that are needed; only in the moment can we shift the dream. This is the work that needs to be done.

The Power of Consciousness

What are these changes that we need to make? How can we change the dream? First we need to understand how our consciousness has created our present situation, and how only a shift in consciousness can redeem our world.

It is our attitude of separation—our belief that we are separate from the world we walk in, that spirit and matter are separate—that has created the dying, polluted world in which we live and which we are about to leave to our children and grandchildren. A shift into a consciousness that sees life as a living, dynamic, interconnected whole of which we are a part, a 'consciousness of oneness', is needed if we are to heal and transform our world.

Behind our present ecological self-destruction, caused by industrial pollution, by the chemicals, toxins and particularly carbon that our civilization emits, lies our desire for material progress, the demon of consumerism and greed that walks with heavy boots over the sacred soil of our world. At the root of our predicament is a deep disregard for the environment and for the consequences of our actions, until it is too late. This is the product of a consciousness that is cut off from the natural world and its interconnectedness. It comes from an attitude that we are separate from the world around us and can do with the world what we want—an attitude that is unthinkable to indigenous people who respect and revere the physical world, and whose cultures protect the balance between humanity and nature.

Our Western consciousness evolved through the birth of scientific reasoning to treat the physical world as a mere object, something mechanical whose laws we could learn and thus master. We developed the gifts of science, but also began to create the materialistic wasteland that we now inhabit. We banned the symbolic world as mere superstition, and the understanding of the relationship between the worlds that linked together all of creation, the concept of the 'Great Chain of Being' was forgotten. Rather than being part of an interdependent whole, each part nourishing and supporting the other, we became lords of a soulless earth, which we sought to dominate and subjugate for our own ends.

Underlying this outlook is a deep, patriarchal conditioning. As our collective consciousness shifted from a matriarchal understanding of the world as a living sacred being, the divine became a transcendent God, living in heaven. The sacred streams and groves became just the stuff of myth, the nature spirits that inhabited them forgotten. Patriarchal consciousness excluded the divine from the natural world, whose darkness man then had to conquer. We were left alone in the world with a God we could only experience after death. Living in a world without the presence of the divine, we had only our own laws to follow, our own desires to nourish us. The results of this consciousness can be seen in our ecological devastation and the soulless world of our materialistic dreams.

And yet there is another quality of consciousness that is now being offered to us, a consciousness of interconnectivity and oneness. This consciousness is not just a spiritual ideal, but a tangible reality expressed in the global connectivity of the Internet and cell-phone networks. We are one, interconnected whole, from the cyber cafes in Uzbekistan to the cell phones of Somalia. And just as the consciousness of separation gave us the benefits and pollutants of science, the dawning consciousness of oneness can give us the vision and knowledge that we need to heal and transform the world.

If we bring into our daily awareness the knowing that we are all a part of one living whole that is interconnected like the cells of our own body, we will discover that the world can change in unexpected ways. This has to do with the magic and power of oneness, how a single living organism can change and evolve more quickly and in ways unavailable to a multitude of separate organisms. But sadly, although we live with the gift of this new paradigm in the form of the Internet and global communication, we have not brought its implications into our consciousness. We have not dared to leave behind defined laws of our Newtonian consciousness or the self-defensive patterns of egotistic self-interest. We have not stepped from 'me' to 'we'. And so we are left with the debris of a dying civilization, hoping that some technological miracle can save us, while our politicians argue about short-term economic progress.

The Possibilities of a Moment

A prophecy can be interpreted in many different ways. To a consciousness caught in a world that is fixed and definable, the interpretation of a prophecy is an attempt to predict what will happen. A more fluid consciousness sees in a prophecy the possible potency of a particular moment in time. One of the esoteric truths that we have forgotten is that some moments are more potent, more full of possibilities than others. We know this in the rhythm of the tides, how there are moments when the water comes closer to the shores. We know that in the movement of the heavens there are moments when the planets or the stars are aligned in a particular way. Astrology seeks to understand the meaning of these alignments, while the poet eloquently writes:

> There is a tide in the affairs of men
> Which, taken at the flood, leads on to fortune;
> Omitted, all the voyage of their life
> Is bound in shallows and in miseries.[1]

We all know how there are moments in our own lives that open the doors to change: a chance meeting, a job offer, even reading a particular book. How we respond to the possibilities of a particular moment may define our life, whether we move into the future that is offered in that moment, or stay in the past. Just as there are moments in the life of an individual, there are also moments in the life of the whole. These are the moments when the forces in the inner and outer world are aligned to help the world to make a step, though their energy can also bring disaster.

There are specific moments in the destiny of the planet: one only has to think of an asteroid striking the earth, or a volcano erupting. But there are also other moments in our cosmic time that, rather than bringing destruction, offer the potential for transformation; for example, the birth of Christ that was imaged in the new star seen by the Wise Men. What matters is how humanity responds to these moments and whether we have been attentive to the stars or listened to the voices crying in the wilderness as ways that can prepare us for such moments.

The signs are all around us that such a moment is near. There is a deep anxiety that is beginning to surface within our collective Western consciousness, that life, as we know it, cannot continue. Forces are building up in the inner and outer worlds. Those who listen to their dreams and the dreams of others have seen the tsunami coming, the dark clouds gathering on the horizon, as well as seeing images of a new future, a return to the sacred and the simple joy of life. One does not need a prophecy to know that something has to change. But as the fault lines beneath our feet begin to shift, it can be helpful to know that such a moment could be near. There is a pressure building up that needs us to be awake, that needs us to listen and watch in the inner and outer worlds.

Has the Mayan prophecy of 2012 caught our attention because we know that a moment either of disaster or of transition is coming? Is the prophecy real or just an image that has focused our attention, and does it matter? The Mayan calendar speaks about the end of time. Does this mean that we will experience the end of our civilization, the doomsday scenario Hollywood would present to us, or does it mean that we can step into a moment that is alive with a new quality of consciousness—the simple timeless joy of life that will be given back to us? A prophecy often has many possibilities, but what is important is that this prophecy has attracted our attention, caught our imagination, and speaks a language that touches us with both a promise and a threat. Maybe we have misread what it says, have not grasped its real meaning. But it calls us to take notice. And always, what really matters is how we respond: whether we embrace the new consciousness that is being offered or stay with the patterns of the past.

II.
A Personal Vision and Prayer

So far, I have presented an objective scenario of this present time. I have described the crisis of our present era, and how a different quality of consciousness is dawning within us. I have called this 'the consciousness of oneness' and suggested that it has the potential to change our present global predicament, open the doorway to a different way of living together with each other and the planet. And I have suggested that, although this consciousness can only be born in the moment, not at some specific time in the future, there are moments in cosmic time that can help us to realize our potential—help us to make the transitions that are needed. And often times of crisis are also times of possibility and real change. Whether this assessment of our present global situation relates directly to the Mayan prophecy I do not know, but the prophecy does focus our attention on a not-too-distant future.

However, this draws me into a more personal assessment of the forces at work in the inner and outer world. Over the last thirty years I have closely watched certain forces constellate, certain patterns evolve. It began when I was working in the archetypal world, a reality long known to the shaman. Here I experienced how certain archetypal patterns were changing, certain forces were awakening. Carl Jung describes these archetypal forces as the great determining factors within humanity, their patterns the 'river beds' through which the waters of life flow. When these forces begin to shift in the depths, one knows that something in the core of humanity is changing.

As these forces began to shift, old patterns of power began to fall away and a new archetype emerged. This archetype appeared to me in the image of the cosmic child with stars in its eyes. And this child described itself as a space rather than a form, a sacred space in which we can be our true selves and experience the joy that belongs to life itself. The new archetype is a possibility that is free of many of the restrictions of the past, and it also has a magic that enables things to happen in a way they have never happened before. It is alive in a completely new way and it is born not from the past but from the moment that is outside of time and yet fully present.

I began to become aware of how much we have restricted ourselves, imprisoned our human potential in the forms of our rational conditioning. And coming alive within the depths of humanity was a new way to be, a way that returns us to the sacred core of our being and its magical potential. If we have access to this archetypal energy, many of the toys of triviality that we use to distract and entertain us will no longer be needed. Once again, we can be nourished directly by life and its inherent joy. And in this reconnection are many possibilities for healing both our planet and ourselves. We would again be given access to the magic within creation.

And then I saw the darkness that surrounds us now, and how it does not want something so precious to be given so freely. I saw how we are controlled by the forces that manipulate us into greed, that create the web of desire that holds us in the grip of this consumer society that is poisoning our souls and the planet. These forces can be seen at work within the multinational companies that control so much of the buying and selling we call life, and yet they come from a deeper place within creation, a place that does not want any change, that does not want the light. These forces are ancient and powerful; they know cunning and deceit and how to sell our souls for a few pieces of silver. They offer us the image of progress even while they deny us the sacred light that alone can nourish our souls and our daily life. And they are feeding off the life-blood of the planet.

Not only do they draw us into this web of wanting, but they also make sure that we remain unfulfilled, addicted to the products that promise so much and give so little. And these forces are even more dangerous because they are covering the world in forgetfulness, the forgetfulness of our divine nature. How can we reconnect with our soul when we have forgotten we have a soul? How can we reclaim our divine nature when we have forgotten we are divine? The forces of forgetfulness are very powerful and we are so easily seduced by the false sweetness we are offered. We become indentured servants selling their products, not even knowing the light we have left behind.

And then I was taken into the very core of creation, and saw that the shift that is being offered to humanity and to the whole world comes only every thousands of years. This is not just the shift into a new age, but into a way of being that has not been offered for many millennia. And the world is included in a way that it has not been since the beginning, since the early days when consciousness was given to humanity and everything was sacred. This time is just a distant memory in our collective consciousness, a time 'before the fall', which we retain as an image called paradise when we walked in the Garden of Eden together with God. This was a time before time, when humanity was not separate from the sacred, when the simplicity and directness of our divine nature were present in every breath, in every step. Sometimes, even today, one can encounter children who still live for a few years in this magical world, before the coldness of our competitive culture freezes them out of its warmth. But I was shown that humanity had the possibility to claim this connection once again, to no longer live in separation, to no longer live in exile.

And then I was reminded that there was a time when the heart of the world was awake and sang the song of creation. And I heard this ancient song that brought tears to my own heart, and I knew that if the heart of the world started to sing, all of creation would come alive in a new way, that it would be like spring at the end of thousands of years of winter. And I saw how the sacred colors would return, and birds of remembrance would sing, and how we could reconnect with all the different creatures of the earth and know their language and their ways, and once again live in harmony with all of creation. It is so long since the heart of the world has sung that we have even forgotten it in our mythological memory. There are traces of it in the Australian aboriginal song lines through which the aboriginal people find their way through the bush. However, we do not even know that the world has a heart, let alone that the heart can sing. But there is the possibility for this song to return, for the world to awaken again. Then we will know what it really means to be alive.

And I saw the places of power that belong to the future, waiting to be awakened, waiting for their energy to be activated. The power of places like Stonehenge lies in eras of the distant past, but there are new places waiting whose energy belongs to the next step in our human evolution, places that will bring together the energies of heaven and earth in a new way, and use the sacred power that belongs to both. So much was shown to me in the inner worlds, the light and the darkness. And I saw small groups of mystics and seekers holding a new light for humanity, forming a web of light around the world. They have neither structure nor organization; they do not even know how they are linked together. But they are part of the organic structure of the light body of the planet, helping in its evolution, so different from the hierarchical, organized forces of darkness that are so visible. And I saw how a thread of divine remembrance was being woven into the light body of the planet, and how this could help in healing the planet. And how the darkness was always trying to divert our attention, to take us back to the ego and the curse of consumerism.

And so the drama of our world continued to be played out through the weeks and months and years; and the world was dying, and the soul of the world was crying for help. And some souls were responding to this call and others were caught in forgetfulness. And the heart of the world was waiting.

On the world stage there were wars and the actions of terrorists, a stock market bubble and a real estate and banking collapse. And all the time within creation, a light was trying to be born, and some souls were drawn to act as midwives, to help it to be born. I saw in my prayers and meditations that there was a new note in the love at the core of creation, and that this note of love had not been played before, and that it has a meaning for the far distant future. And I saw how the darkness was gathering its forces to make sure that nothing new could be born. As always, the destiny of humanity in this world is played out between the forces of light and darkness, but at this time of transition this contest of forces is emphasized. While the light and the love struggle to give us our divine heritage, our freedom and joy, the darkness finds new ways to distract us and to deny the light its power. And I saw more and more clearly that humanity could not make this transition alone. It has been too long since it knew about the workings of the inner worlds. Its shamans and seers have almost all gone. We have forgotten the places of power and the sacred words. Instead, we are left with a few new-age teachings, which may bring us some light but have little understanding of the forces in creation.

And so we are left waiting in the gathering darkness. Slowly, the light of the last age is going out. Slowly, the meaning of life is being lost, until, as in Shakespeare's Macbeth:

Life's but a walking shadow...
...It is a tale
Told by an idiot, full of sound and fury,
    Signifying nothing.[2]

Like Macbeth, we have killed our king, our sacred self, for the values of the ego, not really knowing what this means until the light goes out, and we know only the wasteland of the inner and outer worlds.

Is this the doom that 2012 is foretelling? Is this the prophecy we are being given? This is far worse than any Hollywood image, far bleaker and more enduring. And life without light, without meaning or purpose, is what we have created or been drawn into. And yet there is always another possibility; hope has not yet gone. The prayers of the world could be answered and 2012 could be a time when more light is given, when the heart of the world wakes up and throws off the dust and the darkness.

There is an ancient prophecy that at a time of real crisis, not just a physical disaster, but a crisis on the level of the soul, divine intercession is possible.[3] Many people have experienced this within their own life, how a time of despair and darkness becomes a moment of grace. But we have forgotten that what happens to an individual could happen to the whole world. We have mythic memories of the flood when an angry God sought to destroy the darkness, but we do not know what it might mean for the power of divine light to intercede. We have forgotten about the power of God. It is not even present in our prophecies.

But this is a real possibility, and one that I pray for. As a mystic, I know what it means for a fragment of This Power to come into my heart and into my life: how it can change everything in a moment. I know the absolute reality of This Presence and how the forces of darkness cannot withstand It. Is it not time to welcome the Divine back into this world, to open the door of our hearts and the whole world for our Creator and Beloved? There will be a price to pay for our forgetfulness, as we finally take responsibility for our ego-centered culture that has ravaged the world. Maybe this is one of the reasons why we hide from the light. But 'His mercy is greater than His justice' and how can the world be reborn without the presence of divine Light?

From my own inner experience I know that only the Divine can affect real transformation, and that This Presence is needed to heal the world. We have done so much damage to ourselves and to the world, and the forces of darkness have hidden us from the light. We have denied the sacred within our self and within the world. We do not have the knowledge or power to change our world.

Although many shifts and changes have taken place in the inner worlds, we appear to be lacking the energy to bring them to the surface, to live them in our collective consciousness. We still live in a world of separation even when we know that oneness is all around us. We are surrounded by decay rather than the joy of a new birth. I pray that 2012 offers a real moment of Divine Presence so that we can begin to live the possibilities that are waiting within us and within the world.

1   Shakespeare, *Julius Caesar* Act 4, scene 3, 218 - 221
2   *Macbeth*, Act 5, scene 5, 24-28
3   This is similar to Krishna's prophecy in the Bhagavad Gita, Book 4, verse 7
     'Whenever dharma declines and the purpose of life is forgotten, I manifest myself on earth.'

Chapter Four

The Living Prophecy: Exploring the Mystery of 2012

Eden Sky

First and foremost, if there is one thing I can assuredly say about 2012, it is that: *We are The Prophecy.* Our lives are the creative ground on which the transformation of worlds is taking place. Right now, through our intentions and actions, each of us is directly contributing to the one planetary equation that determines the quality of our collective expression of life on Planet Earth. The decisions we make in these very moments are of critical importance. From the way we wield our emotions, to the details of our lifestyle choices, to how we direct our creative energies, it is crucial we sincerely understand that we are impacting all of life, even beyond the scope of our own personal lifetimes. At this point in the grand cycles of time, within this living garden of life, we must all heed the call to compost the old ways and focus on nurturing the potent seeds of new growth.

As a planetary society, we are in a great initiation process, living through an unprecedented time of instability, mutation, and opportunity emerging on all levels—physically and spiritually. This moment on Earth has never existed before as it does right now. Our human population is climbing off the charts, accelerating by the day, as are the environmental crises, species extinctions, and the vast whole-system struggles of peoples worldwide. We are experiencing a tension of the opposites playing out between contracted forces of fear that seek to have false power by manipulating life with a mind founded in duality, and the expansive forces of possibility that seek to be empowered by living in harmony with life. We are in a great in-between time right now, where we feel and see the manifestation of great extremes. The old world mentality, founded in separation, greed, and unconscious consumer materialism has reached dangerous peaks.

Simultaneously, never before has there been so much possibility at our fingertips. A new way of being is trying to emerge in our world, through our hearts and minds, like a flower determined to grow through the cracks in the cement. New comprehensions and new solutions are emerging and taking root—from new sciences, to new economic models, new healing modalities, new energy technologies, new educational models, new forms of conflict resolution, etc. These times of crisis are unifying us and catalyzing us to awaken to our personal and collective responsibilities as collaborators in this one cauldron of creation.

As we look to the clues held within the ancient prophecies, it is humbling and enlightening to realize they were left specifically for those of us alive *today*, to inspire and assist us in courageously finding our way through these precarious moments. Having studied these cryptic keys for the past fifteen years, I celebrate the context they have given me. From them, I understand that it is essential we do not become discouraged by the increasing intensity of our journey, but rather that we know these times are accelerated on purpose. Indeed, we are right on schedule—in the most cosmic sense of the unfolding timing of our evolutionary processes.

It is not solely the prophecies of the Ancient Maya that speak of the Shifting of World Age Cycles and the resultant transition from one dominant era of consciousness to the next. One can find mention from many indigenous peoples, religions and traditions around the globe that affirm we are now living in landmark times in the history of our planet, in which the entire orientation and mentality of our species and our way of living on Earth, is being restructured and realigned to make way for a new era to dawn.

It is said by many that the quickening process we are currently in will continue ramping up its force, and that the great challenges and immense obstacles will likely continue surmounting as we deepen in this internal and external process of shifting Ages. The Hopi say we are living in *The Time of Great Purification*. These simple words invoke vast meaning. They say we are closing the Fourth World Age of Destruction, preparing to enter the Fifth World of Peace. This is now the time to embrace all that has been dishonored or denied, for it is emerging to be purified and sanctified. All that is manifesting on the inner and outer planes reflects the sacred opportunity of these prophetic times. Accountability is required on all levels of our existence. An essential theme of this prophecy is *becoming conscious of all that has been unconscious*.

What's Going to Happen in 2012?

In our collective consciousness, '2012' has become an inkblot upon which humans have projected the full spectrum of our hopes and fears. One can find countless theories about what's supposed to happen—ranging from all out doom and gloom, to total enlightenment and ascension, to absolutely nothing. It is important to look beyond the hype, and to be aware that many of the predictions now in circulation have no roots in the actual prophecies of the ancients. There are suggestions from A-Z of what Solstice 2012 is signifying—from a new era of telepathic unification and the start of a new cycle guided by a sensitivity to our interdependence with all of nature, to a time of great cataclysms with huge loss of human life, vast flooding, volcanic eruptions, solar flare storms, pole shifting, another ice age, etc. It seems these elements are part of the same story, as the forces of destruction and creation together dance our world into being.

It is wise for us to become increasingly lucid and willing instruments for new possibilities of a new world era to descend.

However, it is essential we do not naively focus on 12/21/2012 as though it will bring instant resolution to all our far-reaching global problems. No one can say with any certainty what will or will not happen precisely on that Solstice day, nor how gradually or rapidly all the changes yet to come will unfold. We must genuinely comprehend that this process of shifting cycles is a journey we are all engaged in, right now. We are already living through a time of unspeakable intensity, on the edge between extinction and illumination. There is nothing to wait for. *This is the time to do the work of our life's awakening that is blatantly in front of us.*

As we take our attention off the 2012 date as being some linear point in the future that some event is going to happen that determines our fate, we can understand this prophecy is an unfolding adventure, a mysterious quest revealing itself through the fabric of our lives. Rather than expecting some product or circumstance that will arrive on a particular day and time, we can see this prophetic date for what it really is: a reminder from the Ancients that *these are the critical moments to bring our inspiration and empowerment to the fore.* We must all take our places in transforming our human culture to be one of Harmony—conscious connectivity with ourselves, with each other and with all of Nature.

Although the actual physical events of the day December 21, 2012 may fall short of people's fantastical projections, the fact is that this date has gained the world's attention, and surely will bring the focus and participation of the greatest number of people together in all of history! Depending on how we all meet the opportunity, we may find its whole purpose is to unify our minds in awareness of each other, and all life throughout the planet and the cosmos. The 2012 synchronization of our attention may indeed catalyze the dawning of a new era of telepathic unification that may deepen over generations to come.

As we take into account the findings of quantum physics,

which prove the effect of the observer on the observed, we can recognize there is great power in how we each conceive of 2012 and what we project onto it, knowing that our perceptions, beliefs and attitudes have an immense influence on generating our experience of reality.

Ultimately, it is a sacred challenge and honor to be alive and participating in these exciting times. An important point made by Mayan Ajq'ij Carlos Barrios, regarding the warnings from the ancients of possible catastrophes yet to come, is that it is critical we realize that it is within our power to change the outcome. He says it is within our power to prevent the worst-case self-destruction scenarios from happening, and instead rise to a new level of evolution.

In this time of 'The Closing of the Cycle', we are living in a great unknown. One can amass endless opinions, data, and theories, but ultimately there are no outside authorities to turn to for guidance. There are no experts that can guarantee anything about our future. No one truly knows what is in store for us, because it depends on how we all navigate from this here and now, how we collectively respond to all the elements life brings, and how our human affairs collaborate with the living intelligence of the Earth and Universe we are immersed within. All we have is this moment; this is the moment of power. *To truly know how to navigate these critical times, we must each find our purest Heart to find our way. The only wise path is to develop our internal discernment: our faculties of intuition and direct communication with our own higher self, with our spiritual guides, and with the living Earth itself.*

What's on the Other Side of 2012?

According to the world's supreme timekeepers, the December 21, 2012 date indeed marks the completion of the 5,125-year Great Cycle mapped by the Ancient Maya—formally known as 'The Thirteen-Baktun Long Count'. Delineated as a very specific phase in our human civilization process, the start of this cycle corresponds exactly with the beginning of recorded history in Ancient Mesopotamia. As we endure the closing of this vast, historical era, we can attune to the understanding that a new chapter opens on the other side of it, known by many as 'post-history'.

When we contemplate what the world might be like beyond 2012, let us be clear that no one can predict the specifics of how things may appear as we enter the new cycle, or whether the ongoing macrocosmic and microcosmic transformations may emerge slowly or swiftly, painfully or gracefully.

Realizing that in only a matter of a couple years we will be on the other side of this infamous date, it is not wise to set up December 21, 2012 with expectations. However, as we can honor that on this day, the Ancient 5,125-year Odometer of the Maya resets itself at 13.0.0.0.0, coming back to its sacred Zero point, we can see Solstice 2012 as a gateway that marks entrance into a new cycle—one that shall indeed unfold over generations and generations to come. As we align our intentions and hearts on this auspicious date, let us realize that serving as instruments of a New World Era is a lifetime position that will keep flowering through our dedication, sincerity and discipline to live in harmony with our greatest potential. As Mayan Ajq'ij Carlos Barrios said: 'The change won't happen exactly on this day because it's not changed like a flash of light... [Dec 21, 2012] is just the beginning... It will take years...'

Rather than looking to decipher what physical events may or may not occur with this cycle shifting, we can also relate to 2012 as a code, a symbol, a call that is beckoning and guiding us to look within ourselves and awaken to the higher and deeper dimensions of our being. As Paul Levy shares:

The universe exists in the form of an ever-transforming living symbol of itself, which is to say that it is a continually unfolding, primordial revelation. Just like a dream, the universe is an instantaneous feedback loop, a living work of art, an inspired oracle that is speaking symbolically.

Messages from the Living Maya

Last winter, I had the blessed opportunity to travel to Guatemala, land of the living Maya, and learn firsthand from the land, the peoples, the ancestor spirits who dwell there, and the Maya Priests themselves. In Antigua, a small group of us had the unspeakable honor of participating in sacred Mayan fire ceremony with Grandfather Don Alejandro Cirilo Perez Oxlaj, 13th Generation Quiche Maya Priest and Head of The National Mayan Council of Indigenous Elders in Guatemala, representing 440 Maya tribes. One of the central issues he clarified is that their sacred calendar system was originally given to the Maya Peoples from the four Original Prophets from the Stars. Indeed, the Maya are very confident of the celestial origins of their astounding time science.

After the prayer ceremony, Grandfather Cirilo spoke to the question of 2012. He shared with us that he is hesitant to pinpoint 2012 as the certain date of destiny, for he is weary of putting false claims on the exact timing of a process he knows is in motion. He stated that amongst the Maya of today, they can't collectively say for sure when the cycle is ending because almost all of their calendars and books (and countless sacred artifacts) were brutally destroyed in 1562 by the Roman Catholic Bishop De Landa (only three Maya codices remain intact). According to him, the changes that are supposed to be coming are already happening now and could culminate very soon, or perhaps over the next several generations. He doesn't want the people of the world to have expectations that lead them to say that nothing ended up happening in 2012 and thus discounting the wisdom of the Maya ancestors. Specific dates aside, Grandfather Cirilo offered his perspective that our shift into the new cycle of the Sun will be marked by a time of thirty to seventy hours of prolonged darkness. If this occurs, he stresses the importance of us not fearing this darkness, remaining calm and knowing it will pass.

Grandfather Cirilo's message also points out the supreme necessity for changing our modern ways and taking responsibility for the 'great contamination' that man has perpetuated, so that we can find our way of living in balance with all of creation. He also shares that, for the Maya, this shifting ages is a positive thing that we should be very happy about. From his heart, he implores us to not be afraid in the face of these Unknowns. As Grandfather Cirilo said to us directly, 'Do not be afraid. Do not be afraid. The Children of the Sun will survive'.

He was adamant that the Maya prophecies are not saying the entire destruction of the planet is coming, and the elders are not pleased with the spreading of rumors and misleading information that is creating more fear in the people. As he said, '...it is only a change of a cycle of the Sun. It is not the first time this is going to happen nor will it be the last'.

Depending on who you talk to, one can find evidence that some living Maya definitely endorse the 12/21/12 date as being of critical importance, while some may not be aware of it, or do not necessarily agree with its projected significance. Some think it is a matter for the shamans and priests, and do not relate to the Westernized apocalyptic themes we've married to the 2012 date. The 2009 edition of the traditional Maya Calendar that Grandfather Cirilo was distributing did devote many pages to sharing insights into 'La Profecia Maya 2012', referring to Solstice 2012 as the end of the Thirteen Baktun Cycle.

Realizing the Essential Connection Between Calendars and Consciousness

A calendar is a lens through which we perceive our world. As the ancient Buddhist teaching states: 'As Viewed, So Appears'. The calendars that guide a society create a framework of human perception, and therefore influence human culture. When we look through the lens of the ancient Maya Long Count Calendar, we see that we are nearing the transition from one world epoch to the next. From this vantage, all the signs of this transition are clearly evident. Conversely, when we look through the lens of our modern twelve-month calendar, what do we see? This commonly accepted framework of time has us referencing the days of our lives in terms of the nearest commercial holidays, and whether or not it's a workday or a weekend. What is the date? Oh, it's Saturday, October 24, 2009. This lens highlights that it's supposedly been 2009 years since the birth of Jesus, and (in the United States, at least) we are nearing Halloween, which of course means that Thanksgiving, Christmas and then New Years Day are soon to follow. According to the script, because it's 'Saturday', there is a collective license to party and unwind before heading back to the grind on Monday.

As a global society in great need of self-reflection and transformation, it is important that we ask: does this calendar lens offer us any real inspiration or cosmic direction? Does it remind us of our truest nature or move us to contemplate the meaning and purpose of our lives? Does it guide us to synchronize in harmony with the cycles of the Earth, Moon, Sun and Stars? Does it orient us towards sensing and respecting the sacred nature of all existence? Does it guide us to connect to our deepest potential?

It does not occur to us to expect a calendar to serve in these ways because humanity at large has been conditioned to accept the limitations of the twelve-month calendar, with its linear grid of reality as the only language and reference point for relating to time and navigating its cycles. This is not the only option!

A calendar is a programming device, a daily script we all follow and agree upon, generally without ever questioning its impact. Now that we are nearing the end of this 5,000-year chapter of 'His-story', we are outgrowing the outdated twelve-month program. Established in 1582, and named after Pope Gregory XIII, the twelve-month 'Gregorian' calendar is a product of its predecessors—Julius Caesar's calendar and the earlier Roman Empire calendar. As the first act of globalization, this template of 'mono-time' is the current world standard because of the forceful issuance of this system upon conquered (indigenous) peoples, who lost their lands as well as their religious freedoms to the Vatican's Roman Catholic Church.

Surely, continuing to follow a model of time born of the Roman Empire is not a wise route to establish a new paradigm on Earth. Pages and pages can be written that detail the flaws of this time system, and the effects on our minds and global society resulting from adhering to this archaic calendar. Suffice it to say that the twelve-month Gregorian calendar is not based on logic, science, or nature, and as a dysfunctional measure that is laden with disorder and historical agenda, it keeps us in a fog about the true essence of time. In these times of shifting world ages, we need to realize that a calendar is the central organizing instrument of our global society. As an evolving humanity, we need to transcend the old calendrical confines and look at our time on this Earth through a new lens, a lens that can serve us better at this crucial moment.

In this light, Dr. José Arguelles has declared that an essential message of the 2012 prophecy is the need for humanity to move into a new paradigm by returning to living in natural time. Having invested decades of study into the ancient Maya and their calendars, mathematics, prophecies and cosmology, Dr. Arguelles has determined that humanity is currently operating on an 'artificial timing frequency' that is held in place by the twelve-month calendar and its counterpart, the sixty-minute mechanical clock, called the '12:60 timing frequency'. Arguelles reminds us that we are the only species that is living and operating by a man-made sense of time that has actually placed us apart from—and out of phase with—the rest of the Biosphere.

The mentality engendered by artificial time is summarized by the motto 'Time is Money', keeping us locked into a destructive, materialistic paradigm, to the detriment of the rest of the natural world.

Dr. Arguelles' prescription for returning to harmony and laying the foundation for a new cultural program is to align ourselves with the 'natural timing frequency', called the '13:20 timing frequency', that places us back in phase with the cycles of the Earth and Cosmos, and synchronizes us with our own deepest selves. This 13:20 ratio is the basis of the ancient Mayan mathematics. Dr. Arguelles' prophetic decodings and pioneering efforts, along with the contributions of his former partner, Lloydine Arguelles, have generated a global movement of people in over ninety countries, who are choosing to grow beyond the status quo twelve-month business calendar, and instead utilize the thirteen-Month/twenty-eight-day Natural Time Calendar as the template that frames and informs our perception of time and its sacred unfolding. As a truly life-changing tool, this new time lens is a solar-lunar-galactic calendar that is based on a universal application of the mathematics of the Ancient Maya Time-Science. Rather than being a traditional Mayan calendar that connects one specifically to the culture of the Maya people and their lands, history, ancestry and religion, the thirteen-Month Calendar is specifically designed as a map to guide modern humanity to live in harmony with the natural time frequency, and thus awaken out of our destructive modern paradigm of materialism and disconnection from nature. (See lawoftime.org and 13moon.com to learn more and acquire a calendar.)

Part of the power of this new calendar is that it unites the secular and the sacred. The thirteen-Month calendar offers us a practical way to replace the twelve-month model by giving us a new way to relate to our year cycle and the passing of months and weeks—entirely reorienting our perception of time.

Additionally, it offers another layer of inspiration and guidance known as the 260 different daily 'galactic signatures', which activate our self-reflection and attunement to the synchronistic nature of life. These 260 unique lenses transform our sense of time into a realm of enchantment and exploration. Rather than just labeling today as 'Tuesday', for example, people around the world focus on today as 'Yellow Cosmic Seed', which means the following day will be 'Red Magnetic Serpent', and then 'White Lunar Worldbridger'. This assures that each day will be its own adventure! (A place to start traveling in Natural Time is to decode your own birth-date and find out your galactic signature: www.13moon.com/decoder.htm)

As a synthesis of ancient wisdom and modern revelation, this new calendar is offering us a paradigm to support the unfolding of a new culture that is in phase with the intelligence of nature. As we discover this new language of harmony, we realize that not only are the codes of natural time alive—speaking and revealing themselves through the calendar cycles—but the codes themselves are reflections of nature's codes that live within our own bodies and minds. Children all over the world are learning these natural time codes, proving how easy and fun it can be! As Rita Pitka Blumenstein, one of The Thirteen Indigenous Grandmothers said: 'If we understand the Thirteen, the world will become balanced'.

Returning to Natural Time

While the modern world measures time with machines and grids, boxing and dissecting our time into little, repeating, blank, bland squares that we call days and mechanized moments we separate into hours and minutes and seconds, our timeless souls long to be liberated into the organic expanse of nature's pulse. This pulse lives within us; our heart beats naturally in synch with the rhythms of creation.

We are being called to evolve beyond our man-made artificial versions of time—and instead utilize a new calendar that will assist us in having a new mindset as we close this cycle of history and prepare for the possibilities of post-history. The thirteen-Moon/twenty-eight-day calendar is actively in use around the world, by people who are choosing to break the spell of artificial time and participate in the fulfillment of prophecy!

As we reawaken to the magic of Nature's timing, let us learn how to be in the clock world, but not of it. While the clock may fill a current need as a societal tool, let us be wise in how we let it dominate or dictate our rhythms. Let us be willing to slowly but surely take our power back from the clock world, weaning ourselves from our reliance on it, making space in our minds to sense our own natural rhythms. It is important to note that the clock was the first automatic machine—going on to become the heart of all machine technology to come. The presence of the clock gave birth to the notion that time lies outside our bodies— replacing the guiding rhythm of our heartbeat with the ceaseless tick-tock of the wristwatch. As a six-year old girl once declared, 'The clock wants to turn everybody into a machine'.

The adherence to the clock for our sense of time and timing is noted as the greatest obstacle to allowing the full telepathic abilities of the human to flower. As George Woodcock wrote in 1944:

> ...because, without some means of exact time keeping, industrial capitalism could never have developed and could not continue to exploit the workers, the clock represents an element of mechanical tyranny in the lives of modern men more potent than any individual exploiter or any other machine... Now the movement of the clock sets the tempo men's lives—they become the servant of the concept of time which they themselves have made, and are held in fear, like Frankenstein by his own monster.

As we learn to live in phase with the harmonic ratios of Natural time, we can hear our own higher self inform us through our intuitive sense of timing. Ultimately, this Living Prophecy is calling us to realize that *we* are time. The more we surrender into the natural flow of life's timing, the more directly the natural order of life reveals its patterns, and synchronicities become more conscious!

How Can We Prepare for 2012?

First thing first: rather than focusing on an imaginary destination, we need to realize we are already in the midst of this prophetic unfolding. Likewise, instead of putting all our attention on the old civilization's constructs that are gasping for breath and dying, we might better direct our attention to what is seeking to be born through us, calling to us from the inside, out.

The 2012 synchronization is a call to purpose. On this diverse planet, our strengths, our abilities and our callings differ. What is *our* life's mission? We each have a unique role in these times. We each need to follow our inspiration! As we find our passion, we feel alive, we feel directed. What we need is to feel engaged with life, knowing we are part of this collective mandala of being.

The wisdom of the 2012 code can inspire us to look directly at our lives, right here and right now. What are our guiding principles? What are our motivations? What supports us in feeling truly alive? How can we embody genuine compassion? How can we face our edges and grow? How we can become increasingly aware and self-reflective? How can we deepen our humility? How can we share our talents and gifts as a way to help manifest a new human culture? How can we be of service to life and positively contribute to the Whole? How can we cultivate a balance of being and doing, receptivity and action?

Rather than looking to the world for guidance, it is essential that we learn to hear the voice of our inner wisdom. No one can give us wisdom; wisdom dwells and dawns inside us, born of our own direct experience. We each have our own direct connection to Spirit and we must keep learning how to hear our divine, intuitive directives, whispering within. This ability to hear the voice of our inner guidance is the most practical skill we can cultivate in these times. Synchronicity and telepathy form out of our intuitional voice, steering us to the right place at the right time — reconnecting us thus with the sacred essence of time.

When we look at the state of the world affairs from our rational, linear minds, it is a terrifying scenario that seems inherently doomed with endless causes for alarm and anxiety. But where will those energies of fear and panic get us? They lead to stress, sickness, negativity, depression, self-doubt and escapism, and feelings of being overwhelmed. The old paradigm model uses fear to motivate, whereas the new paradigm is based in allowing our love for life to inspire us. If we can perceive this time of prophecy through our hearts, we can attune to the possibilities of this emerging new world consciousness. How does it want to speak and move through us, touching our relations and rippling out into the world?

As the intensity of our journey continues, it is essential we learn how to work with the presence of fears and practice ways to transmute them so they are not debilitating. As the Shambhala Warrior teachings of Buddhism advise: 'Fearlessness is not about a reduction of fears, it is about feeling the fears but not letting them stop us.'

That is the opportunity of these times — to acknowledge the fears but not let them run us, instead letting their presence guide us back to our tender heart centers. If we can find bravery in our hearts to rise to the great challenges we are in, we can bring beauty and breathe life into possibility.

The Ancient Hawaiians had a prophecy that there would come a time on the planet when there would be so much chaos, it would require many to emerge as 'Agents of Calm'. It feels clear that we have arrived to this point in the cycle! As we focus on cultivating our internal harmony, so we contribute that peace to the world. The more we can practice centering, the better. Meditation and prayer are essential to align our intentions with our clearest self. Likewise, as we deepen our connection with our breath, we find it is the most direct way to ground ourselves in the present moment. Conscious breathing helps us to let go of stress, calm and clear our minds, and reopen to our heart's expanse.

Additionally, to evolve and help the whole of humanity, it is essential that we engage in some form of mind training. As spiritual teacher Alex Polari said, 'Every thought, it is an entity'. We need to be aware of what thoughts we are entertaining, identifying with, energizing and incarnating into life. This is a critical moment to be self-reflective. We must examine everything we can notice about ourselves: our tendencies, our habitual patterns, our attitudes, and what we believe that we believe. *We must question our thoughts.* We must notice the pathways that energy manifests through us. We are just beginning to understand how deeply our perceptions and beliefs mold our experiences of reality.

We must support ourselves holistically in this transformation process we are in. To balance out the artificial energies of these modern times, it is wise to immerse oneself in nature as much as possible. Being in natural environments recharges us with elemental magic and a sense of wholeness that helps to counterbalance the technospheric vibrations and over-stimulation attributable to information overload.

Our bodies are the temples of our spirits; they are the instruments through which we play our life's song. We need to take care of our bodies during these times. We are already living in a compromised situation based on the pollution of the air, water, earth and the increasing electro-magnetic pollution that inundates us from all directions. We must cover all the basics: keeping our bodies vital with movement, rest, water, and organic foods. As Mayan Ajq'ij Carlos Barrios says, 'Eat wisely. A lot of food is corrupt in either subtle or gross ways. Pay attention to what you are taking into your body.'

We must support one another in consciously processing the trauma, challenges and pains of these times. Each of us can help stabilize the chaos in this shifting of world age cycles by continuing to shine the light of awareness into our own inner darkness, bringing healing and illumination to our old wounds and insecurities. It is essential that we find ways and tools that help us release old patterns (rather than projecting them out), so we can be available to the ever-changing present moment. We need to truly learn the powers of forgiveness of self and others, and true mercy towards our human trials and vulnerabilities, learning to be tender towards our relationships and ourselves. Likewise, it is important to face the pain and suffering of our world that is crying out for attention, letting it break our hearts into ever-deepening compassion, opening the channels for more holistic responses.

It is also essential that we have the courage and wisdom to face the reality of our human mortality, accepting the inherent impermanence of all that lives. Rather than living in fear and denial of death, these times are urging us to confront its potency, and to embrace death as a sacred counterpart of the universal equation: an ever-present ally guiding us to live more fully, grateful for *this* precious moment. Contemplating the death of the body and the impermanence of all form also opens us to begin to know the realms of spirit, formlessness, and eternal consciousness—exploring a higher-dimensional context to hold the laws of this physical world within.

Further guidance comes from a Tz'utujil Maya Medicine-Woman from Santiago Atitlan, Guatemala who recently spoke about the importance of relating to Mother Earth, Father Sun and Grandmother Moon as living beings, stating that we need to respect and be in intimate relationship with them. She added that we need to conduct ceremonies, make lots of prayers and give back by making beautiful offerings to Mother Earth, like flowers, incense, and different colored candles. And she stressed that during these times it is important to not be afraid, to be strong, to have faith, to pay attention to our dreams, and to learn how to grow our food gardens.

Many people are aware of the need for us to determine how to live in physically sustainable ways on this planet, but often the issue of spiritual preparation is overlooked. We need both. We definitely need to question the models and values that modern society presents as normal, and increasingly find ways to live that lessen our environmental footprints, especially focusing on developing our local communities. And we also need to purify and align our internal relationship to all of life.

Obviously, as a modern society we are in a whole-systems challenge to reorient our lifestyles to live in harmony with nature. But it is only an illumined understanding of our unity that can truly motivate and guide us to manifest real solutions. While the task at hand may seem insurmountable, let us remain open to possibilities of miraculous breakthroughs emerging, brought about by awakenings in our human consciousness. Let us open to the guidance of new love-based harmonies! As we hold the highest vision for the transformation of our world, rooting to our clearest intentions, let us release expectations on how things are supposed to appear, surrendering to the larger unfolding. Truly, there is no need to impose limits on what might be possible for us as an evolving species; as we move from ignorance to wisdom, greed to compassion, and competition to cooperation, we can discover the untold magic of synergy. *As we recognize that we are enduring a Global Healing Crisis, let us shake off the wounded victim mentality, and arise as Medicine Warriors—here to do the necessary work to help lay the ground for a New Era to root, conscious of our obligations to future generations!*

Finding Our Way: Our Hearts Hold the Keys

This moment in the collective dream is steeped in mystery. This mystery has a heartbeat that lives within us. The mystery blooms in our heart, with petals of innocence and stalks of wisdom. We are each drops in the sea of humanity, part of the physical and psychic collective. Rather than passive spectators, we are here to be conscious participants of this world age transition process. We are all instruments of culture. Our mental, spiritual, emotional and physical energies are the vivid colors splashing on the canvas of Life. What is the quality of our collective art? How can we refine our contribution?

Ultimately, this is no time to try to figure things out with the mind, but rather our task at hand is learning to listen to and respond from the *heart*. We can find a harmonious way through this passage only by finding our hearts. Our heart is naturally attuned to the unity of all life, and therefore lives in respect of it. By finding genuine compassion, we access genuine wisdom.

May we each find our way. May we bring light into the dark, and serve as conscious vehicles of Divine Love. For it is in giving, sharing, inspiring and supporting that this life becomes beautified. We need each other to grieve with, to pray with, to celebrate with. We need to illuminate and uplift each other, over and over, back into connection with our true nature.

Our mission is to manifest a new culture based on conscious, harmonious interconnectedness. This living prophecy is ours to fulfill. We are the living intersection between that which has passed and that which has not yet emerged. We are the dream of our ancestors, and the future memory of generations to come. As we realize our oneness, we uplift our shared dream. The light that shines through my eyes is the same light I see in yours. *As the Maya say: 'In Lak'ech'—I am Another Yourself.*

Chapter Five

2012—The Imminent Emergence

Geoff Stray

Over the last two thousand years, there have been literally dozens of proposed dates upon which the world was expected to end. Around 30 AD, Jesus is reported to have said 'Judgment Day' would come within the lifetimes of his audience. This is the failed prophecy on which all the others were based. However, for hundreds of years before this, the Hebrew people had a tradition of prophecy. Prophets such as Ezekiel and Daniel had predicted that one day the dead would come out of their graves. This concept is preserved in Christianity and Islam, who also expect a Day of Judgment, also known as Yawm al-Ba'th, the day of Rising from the Grave.

There is a lot of talk about 2012 being the latest predicted doom date. However, this one really stands out because all the others for the last 2,000 years have been based on the Bible, whereas this one comes primarily from the calendars and prophecies of the ancient Maya civilization. If we can disconnect ourselves from our Judeo-Christian mindset, then we shall be better able to look at the subject without projecting those patterns onto it.

The Maya lived in an area we now call Mesoamerica—South-East Mexico, and the Yucatan peninsula, Guatemala, Belize, North-West Honduras and North-West El Salvador. In the Classic era of the Maya (250-900 AD), their artistic and cultural achievements reached their height, and this is when they perfected their complex calendar systems. They had a 260-day sacred calendar, the tzolkin, or cholk'ij based around the period of human gestation; a 365-day calendar called the haab; a Calendar Round—a 52-year period after which these two calendars combine—73 tzolkins or 52 haabs; and a Long Count calendar system for recording longer periods of time. There also were other calendars that we don't need to discuss here, except for the 'Short Count' or thirteen-katun cycle, which we shall return to. The Long Count is based around the 360-day year, or tun. There are twenty days in a uinal; eighteen uinals in a tun; twenty tuns in a katun; twenty katuns in a baktun (just under 400 years) and thirteen baktuns in the era.

Over the last hundred years or so, adventurers, archaeologists and anthropologists have attempted to decode the inscribed glyphs that cover the monuments and temples that are slowly being released from the tangled undergrowth. The first glyphs to be decoded concerned the calendar systems, but even so, the understanding of the calendars is still developing. The Long Count calendar incorporates a cycle called the thirteen-baktun cycle, which is 1,872,000 days long—or about 5,125 years. It defines the current era or Creation in which we live.

Around 1900, a newspaper editor and explorer named Joseph Goodman started publishing his translations of the calendar glyphs, and suggested a correlation between the Maya dates and our own calendar. In ensuing years, there have been many other correlations suggested, that put the start-date of the current Creation or era between the extremes of 3392 BC to 2594 BC. Although Goodman and all scholars who followed him knew how many days were in the era and argued over which date in our calendar the start-date corresponds to, it was over half a century before anyone bothered seeing when the end-date might be. In 1950, J. Eric S. Thompson did a huge study, reconsidering evidence from astronomy, inscribed dates on buildings and stelae, dates recorded in the four remaining bark books or codices, plus post-conquest books; dates in the Julian and Maya calendars recorded by the Spanish invaders, and the unbroken tzolkin count still being used in the highlands of Guatemala. The resulting correlation (the GMT-2 or 584283) is now the one that most Mayanists use, and is only three days away from the one first proposed by Goodman fifty years earlier. Some Mayanists use a correlation that differs from this one by two days (the Lounsbury), and one or two still argue for other correlations, but none fulfill so many criteria as the GMT-2.

The start-date that Goodman suggested was equivalent to the 8th August 3114 BC in the Gregorian calendar. Almost everyone referred to the year as '3113 BC' until the 1980s, when it was realized that it was leading to miscalculations because the Gregorian calendar has no 'year zero' — Jesus' birth was said to be in 1 AD and the previous year was 1 BC. Nowadays, a year is added to BC dates to avoid the problem. In 1966, Mayanist Michael Coe published his book, *The Maya*, in which he announced that the current era would end on the 24th December 2011. Unfortunately, this incorporated the one-year error, and it wasn't until 1975 that 2012 appeared in print as the end-point.

There is only one known inscription that mentions the end date. It is monument 6 from Tortuguero, and is damaged and broken. The epigrapher, David Stuart has translated it. Three calendars cross-reference one date:

The thirteenth baktun will be finished on Four Ahau, the Third of Kankin, it (?) will happen. (It will be) the descent of the Nine Support Gods to the (?)

In the GMT-2 correlation, this equates to the 21st December 2012. The Nine gods will return on the zero-day, which is the winter solstice.

In this nine-god complex, the Bolon Yookte' Ku'h are seen as nine individuals or as one god, and the arrival of the Nine gods is echoed in the post-conquest Jaguar Priest prophecies: the Chilam Balam of Tizimin. These prophecies consist mainly of katun prophecies, and the katun is a period of just under twenty years. When the 'Mayan collapse' occurred, and the Classic era finished, the Maya lost their knowledge of the Long Count and just used a thirteen-katun cycle instead. This calendar only covered an era of 260 tuns, or about 256 solar years, so until recently, the katun prophecies were thought to be about events that occurred centuries ago. But Maud Makemson, translator of the Tizimin, found linguistic and calendrical clues that the prophecies, which originally applied to the end of the thirteen-baktun cycle, were retained and reapplied to the thirteen-katun cycle.

> ...in the final days of misfortune, in the final days of tying up the bundle of the thirteen katuns on 4 Ahau, then the end of the world shall come and the katun of our fathers will ascend on high... These valleys of the earth shall come to an end. For those katuns there shall be no priests, and no one who believes in his government without having doubts... I recount to you the words of the true gods, when they shall come. (Tizimin, p.16)

This is the key section of the Tizimin that reveals this as a prophecy for the end of the thirteen-baktun cycle—in other words, 2012. Katuns were named after their final day, and the thirteen-katun cycle ended on katun 13 Ahau. If this was about the end of the thirteen-katun cycle it would say 'the tying up of the bundle of the thirteen katuns on 13 Ahau...' However, it is saying the time-bundle will be complete on 4 Ahau, which is the last tzolkin day in the current katun, which is the end of the thirteen-baktun cycle. Where it says 'thirteen katuns' above, it originally said 'thirteen baktuns,' says Makemson. The current katun is called katun 4 Ahau, because the 21st December 2012 is a 4 Ahau day in the tzolkin. So here we have a prediction of the return of the gods in 2012. In the preceding section, we find the following:

The Nine shall arise in sorrow, alas... And when over the dark sea I shall be lifted up in a chalice of fire, to that generation there will come the day of withered fruit. There will be rain. The face of the sun shall be extinguished because of the great tempest. Then finally the ornaments shall descend in heaps. There will be good gifts for one and all, as well as lands, from the Great Spirit, wherever they shall settle down. Presently Baktun 13 shall come sailing, figuratively speaking, bringing the ornaments of which I have spoken from your ancestors. Then the god will come to visit his little ones. Perhaps 'After Death' will be the subject of his discourse.' (Tizimin p.15-16)

Here, Makemson has translated a phrase as 'Presently Baktun 13 shall come sailing...' again referring to 2012. The Thirteenth Baktun will be completed on 21st December 2012, when the Long Count date reaches 13.0.0.0.0—Mayanists differ as to whether they think the next day will be 0.0.0.0.1 or 13.0.0.0.1. Some think the entire baktun would be numbered thirteen and be followed 400 tuns later by the start of the 'first baktun' on date 1.0.0.0.0. Anyway, we have here a prophecy of the return of the Nine gods, weather effects, disillusionment with governments, something that sounds like a UFO, and a mass near-death experience of some sort.

If we look at Maya mythology, we find stories of past eras. The most famous of these is the Popul Vuh myth, which is the creation myth of the Quiche Maya, but is also represented in Classic Maya art and architecture. It is a long and complex story involving the descent into the underworld of Hun Hunahpu and Vucub Hunahpu (One one-Ahau and Seven one-Ahau or One Hunter and Seven Hunter) to play a ball game with the Lords of Death, Hun Came and Vucub Came—One Death and Seven Death. They are defeated and killed and One Hunter's sons – the

Hero Twins (called One Ahau or just Hunter, and Jaguar Deer), descend to the underworld to exact their revenge. They beat the Lords of death and become immortal.

Encoded into the Popul Vuh myth are past eras, and various commentators disagree as to how many there are. Professor Gordon Brotherston has found that there are five eras encoded. In the first Creation, the people are made of mud, but they were unable to move freely, walk, talk or breed. The gods ended the Creation with a flood. In the second Creation, the 'doll people' were carved from wood, and were stiff and jerky, with no respect. The Creation ended in darkness, with monsters descending from the sky and slashing them with flint knives, and they are attacked by dogs and turkeys. The survivors became monkeys. The third Creation takes place during the second Creation, strangely, and in it, Seven Parrot (or Seven Macaw) and his wife and two sons are selfish and destructive— the parrot has teeth and feathers, like an archaeopteryx and the sons are reptiles, one of whom, Two Leg, sounds like a tyrannosaurus. They are defeated by the Hero Twins. In the fourth Creation, the Hero Twins descend to Xibalba—the underworld, to avenge their father and kill the black and white Death Lords, and limit the boundaries of Xibalba, before ascending into the sky to become the Sun and Moon. In the fifth Creation, Quetzal Snake and companions grind and mould the maize and form the next race of people—the maize people—who are the ancestors of the Quiche.

The theme here, of an evolutionary progression over four past eras, is repeated in other Mesoamerican myths. The Aztec Cauahtitlan Annals describe an initial Sun or era, which was ended by a flood, and people changed into fish. The second Sun ended with an eclipse, when the people were torn to pieces. These sound just like the first two eras in the Popul Vuh. The third Sun ended in a rain of fire or volcanic ash. The fourth Sun ended with a hurricane, and the people turned into monkeys, and the fifth Sun will end in an earthquake.

In the Hopi first World, according to Frank Waters' study, the people communicated telepathically—it was a golden age in which humankind got in touch with the creator through a psychic centre at the top of the head, but they became more self-obsessed and the head centre closed up. Some of those who had avoided the corruption descended into the mound of the Ant people and escaped the destruction, which came in the form of a rain of fire. All went well for a while when they emerged, but eventually, greed spun out of control and led to warfare. Again, those who still lived the unselfish, pure life that was the plan of the creator, escaped into the Ant People's world, while the second World was destroyed by spinning off its axis into space, where it froze over. In the third World, population multiplied. Sexual morality declined, and cities attacked each other with aircrafts (flying shields). This time the pure survivors were sealed inside 'reeds', while the world ended via rain and tidal waves. We are now in the fourth World, or 'World Complete', and if we return to evil ways, Masaw, the ex-underworld guardian, will take the Earth from us again. This scheme seems to be devolving rather than evolving, but the Hopi say there are a total of seven Worlds, and that each is governed by a psychic centre—the same as the top five chakras of the Hindu system. Our consciousness descended from the crown chakra in the first era down as far as the solar plexus in the current era—each era becoming more materialistic than the last—but at the next World era transition, it will start to reverse direction. Each transition is called an Emergence, and is symbolized by a labyrinth symbol—identical to the Cretan labyrinth symbol. It is also known as the Mother Earth symbol, or Mother and Child, and the process is seen as a kind of birth process.

The Zuni, who are close neighbors of the Hopi, say we are in the fifth World, and another Pueblo people, the Navajo, also say we are in the fifth.

In Peru, the descendants of the Inca said we are in the fifth Sun:

The first was lost through water, the second by the sky falling on the earth, which killed the giants that there were, and the bones which the Spaniards have found hidden in various places are theirs... The third sun they say ended through fire, the fourth, through wind; of this fifth sun they had a great account... (Marua, quoted in *Brotherston's Book of the Fourth World*, p.249)

However, some of them have replaced this original version with a sixteenth century Catholic myth of three ages—the Age of the Father, the Age of the Son and the Age of the Holy Ghost.

So we have established that there seems to be an evolutionary transition incorporated into these era transitions, and these transitions are accompanied by extreme weather.

John Major Jenkins has researched the question of why the Maya would target this winter solstice as the end-point of their thirteen-baktun cycle, and has found evidence that the Maya were tracking precession. This is the cycle that we call the precession of the equinoxes, where we say we are currently moving from the age of Pisces to the Age of Aquarius. The earth's axis is about 23 degrees off vertical, and over a period of about 25,800 years it rotates in a complete circle. This causes the position of the celestial pole to move over time, so that we have to allocate a new pole star every thousand years or so. It also means that the constellations are moving slowly in the opposite direction to that in which the Sun, Moon and planets move. On spring equinox, if we measure the slow movement of the constellation that is behind the Sun (even though we can't see it), we find that Pisces is slipping back at a rate of one degree every 72 years. Well, it seems the Maya were measuring this same cycle, but measuring from the winter solstice position instead of the spring equinox. The thirteen-baktun cycle consists of 5,200 tuns or 360-days years. Five eras of this length amounts to 26,000 tuns—an entire precession cycle.

Between 1980 and 2016, the winter solstice sun is crossing the galactic equator. This is encoded in Maya myths (including the Popul Vuh), and in their ball game, in the art and inscriptions and in the alignments of their buildings. Caves represent the location of the Maya underworld, in the daytime, but at night, Xibalba be, the black road to the underworld, is right there on the galactic equator—the dark patch that astronomers call the Dark Rift. The rebirth of One Hunahpu—the dead father of the Hero Twins—is depicted (on stone carvings from Izapa) being reborn in the mouth of the jaguar toad. The god is the solar deity, and the jaguar toad's open mouth represents the Dark Rift. This is what Jenkins calls, 'galactic alignment'. In this way, the Maya saw the coming era transition as a kind of rebirth—the birth of a new Sun, as did the Inca.

Admittedly, 2012 is not the centre of this process—that was around 1998, but it seems that the Maya deliberately targeted the winter solstice of 2012 as the significant focus point in the 36-year window of galactic alignment. At this time, the earth's axis has come into alignment, so that on winter solstice, it is pointing in the direction of the galactic bulge—the fat central part of the Milky Way, where the Dark Rift is—the visual centre of the galaxy (the actual centre is just off the ecliptic and the Sun will not be in conjunction with that for about another 200 years, but any galactic field effects will manifest along the galactic equator). So it could be that the earth's magnetic field is interacting with the galactic field, but why in 2012 and not 1998?

The answer to this could be that some other factor will trigger the effect. One possibility is the record-breaking solar-magnetic effects that have been predicted by NASA to occur in 2012, at solar maximum. Every eleven years or so, the Sun's magnetic field reverses and at solar maximum, solar activity is at its highest. Over the last few years, the Sun has been getting more active, with larger flares, faster solar wind, and more consequent effects on earth's magnetic field, moving the Northern Lights to lower latitudes, and causing power blackouts. The recent lack of sunspots has now been explained—they were occurring at a deeper level, and the projected solar maximum for 2012 still persists.

This is one possible factor that might cause an overloading effect at the time of earth and galactic field interaction—a solar switch. There are some scientific findings that support the possibility that our orientation to the centre of the galaxy can have profound effects on us. One of these is to be found in the results of Professor Simon Shnoll, after decades of research into biochemical reaction rates and radioactive decay rates. He found that instead of a smooth bell-curve, the results did not average out, but produced certain spikes. These correlated to the sidereal day, sidereal year, and to a short sunspot cycle. In other words, our orientation to the stars (and all the visible stars are in this galaxy) affects our biochemistry. The second factor is from the work of James Spotiswoode, who found that in experiments with extra-sensory perception there is a huge jump in people's abilities when Galactic Centre appears on the horizon. So, perhaps some kind of field interaction could cause a huge jump in human paranormal abilities and changes to our biochemistry and neurochemistry.

This possibility fits in with the predictions that have come from contemporary people all over the world, who have returned after altered states of consciousness, such as near-death experiences, alien abduction, out-of-body states, lucid dreams, remote viewing, experiences with sacred plants, and even deep trance meditation. They are all predicting a huge jump in human consciousness, accompanied by earth changes in 2012.

In 1975, Dannion Brinkley was speaking on the telephone

when a thunderbolt hit the phone line and he was thrown physically into the air. He found himself floating above his body, until, in the ambulance, his heart stopped for twenty-eight minutes and he was propelled down a tunnel, emerging into a bright light. In the presence of a bright silver being, he had a life-recall experience in which he relived all the times in his life when he had affected others, and he felt the pain and joy he had given them—a classic self-judgment process. Following this, he was taken to a crystal city, where he was shown over a hundred scenes from the future—major world events that have nearly all come to pass in the intervening years. These included the Gulf War, the explosion of the Chernobyl nuclear facility, the fall of the Berlin Wall, technological breakthroughs and climate change. His visions concluded with seeing an escalation of earth changes that coincide with 'the return of an energy system that existed here a long time ago', and that this will be particularly focused on 2011 – 2012. Then, between 2012 and 2014 there will be a geomagnetic reversal, and the whole scenario will present a spiritual consciousness-raising opportunity for humankind.

In 1998, a totally independent theory from a Siberian Geologist named Alexey Dmitriev was published, and it seems to uncannily echo Brinkley's predictions. Dmitriev notes in his paper, *The Planetophysical State of the Earth and Life,* that there are magnetic and atmospheric changes throughout the whole solar system, not just on earth, and that these (as well as the increased solar activity) seem to be connected to a huge build-up of interstellar plasma that has collected on the edge of the heliosphere (the edge of the solar system, where the solar wind meets interstellar space). The outer planets seem more affected, with Uranus and Neptune having had approximate 50-degree alterations in their magnetic fields. Dmitriev says the solar system is becoming embedded in a cloud of plasma, which is triggering these changes (plasma is the fourth state of matter, after solids, liquids and gases—a charged electron cloud), and that they will culminate in 'the spontaneous mass evolution of humanity as we now know it'. He also says that it will trigger a geomagnetic reversal, as the increased influx of magnetized plasma interacts with our geomagnetic field.

This coincidence between the 1975 NDE visions of Brinkley and the scientific theory from Siberia two decades later suggests that we may be looking at a potential explanation for the convergence of ancient prophecies in a window area around 2012.

John Major Jenkins has also published a book called *The Pyramid of Fire*, in which he tracks down a lost Aztec codex that proves what has been speculated by various researchers over the years, that the religion of the Toltecs—based around Quetzalcoatl, the feathered serpent god, known to the Maya as Kukulcan—was originally about the concept of an evolutionary energy that lies dormant at the base of the human spine. The concept is almost identical to the Hindu concept of Kundalini— the fire serpent that can be released from its slumber and raised up the spine, energizing the power zones or charkas, until it reaches the crown chakra.

Here we have a connection to the prophecies of the Chilam Balams that mention a return of the gods in the katun 4 Ahau that ends the thirteen-baktun cycle, specifically, the Chilam Balam of Chumayel that says in katun 4 Ahau, Kukulcan will return. The twenty-year period we are now in, until December 2012, is katun 4 Ahau (the 'katun of dishonor'). This suggestion of a mass movement of kundalini is echoed in the Hopi prophecy mentioned earlier, which predicts that in the Emergence to the Fifth World, consciousness starts to move up from the solar plexus to the heart. In Kundalini lore, it is said that when kundalini reaches the Anahata or heart chakra, the soul awakens.

So, in this short look at ancient calendars and prophecies, we have seen that the Maya saw 2012 as a new Creation, when the gods will return; many sources foresee increased climate changes; there is a suggestion of a rebirth experience; a mass spontaneous evolution; a raising of consciousness; a near-death experience; a widespread Kundalini experience; a jump in paranormal abilities. This emergence of the next sub-species of human is the Earth's final hope; that its cancerous organ— humanity—will finally be metamorphosed in the nick of time, from an all-devouring caterpillar into its higher function as a cooperative, telepathic, compassionate earth-lover—perhaps even (as Peter Russell suggests) the global neo-cortex.

Chapter Six

What the Maya Tell Us About 2012

Dr. Mark Van Stone

The short version: Don't cash in your IRA; don't quit your job. It's not the end of the world.

(But DO tell that co-worker what you *really* think of his cologne!)

The ancient Maya produced a rich and fascinating culture, and, despite rumors to the contrary, they have not 'disappeared'. The six million Maya living in Guatemala, the Yucatán, and neighboring territories are alive and, well, persisting. Though ruled by invaders, relegated to second-class citizenship, their spirit is indomitable.

The first thing that attracted me was their calligraphy. Voluptuous, enticing, mysterious, Maya hieroglyphs are as riotous, crowded and curvaceous as Egyptian is disciplined, spare and lean. Jungle contrasted with desert. Then, too, the ancient Maya are surrounded by mystery: the collapse of their civilization, their awesome lost cities, their sophisticated astronomy and mathematics, and most of all their then undeciphered hieroglyphs[4]. This inscrutable culture inspires and fires the imagination. Indeed, our very ignorance is what permits so many fantasies, fears, and hopes to be projected upon it. Here be dragons.

A *Very* Brief Introduction to the Maya Calendars

The one part of Maya inscriptions we *did* work out early (about 1900) was the intricate machinery of their calendars. Like us, they had a 365-day year divided into 'months' with numbered days, called the *Haab*. Like us, they measured linear time from a fixed initial date, called the *Long Count*.[5] We also have a repeating seven-day cycle, which runs concurrently with the other two. The Maya 'week', however, is much more complex, a 260-day cycle consisting of two smaller interlocked cycles: one of thirteen numbers and another of twenty named days. As with our calendars, the Maya inherited these three reckonings[6] from earlier peoples, who invented them in different times and places, for different purposes. Like our week, the Maya 260-day cycle or *Tzolk'in* ('count of days') was by far the oldest calendar. Like our week, the *Tzolk'in* has no relationship with the solar or agricultural rhythms; its origin lies in magic and augury. Like our week, the days of the *Tzolk'in* are animate, alive, with varied character: 'Monday's child is fair of face, Tuesday's child is full of grace, Wednesday's child is full of woe...[7]'

Despite their stone-age technology, Maya numbers vie with Babylonian as the most sophisticated in the ancient world.[8] Ancient and a few modern Maya count much as we do, using the concepts of place-value and zero; they and their neighbors probably employed the zero earlier than anyone else in the world. (However, since their hot climate compelled them to wear sandals or go barefoot, they count in base-twenty, rather than our hands-only base-ten.) This system allowed, indeed it *encouraged* them to manipulate very large numbers. This they did with relish; one important hieroglyphic text (*Palenque Temple of Inscriptions West Tablet*, ca. AD 683) connects two events 1,246,826 years and some days apart. Another inscription (the fourth-century jade *Leiden Plaque*) indicates the extraordinary emphasis they placed on Time: its date (in the various Maya calendars) occupies over 75 per cent of the inscription. It seems that specifying its moment in time was more important than *the coronation itself*. This unique emphasis on precise time intervals and dates (plus the fact that the rest of the glyphs resisted decipherment for a century) convinced some twentieth-century epigraphers that the Maya worshipped Time itself. Indeed, even now, when we now know better, we still marvel at their obsession with fixing events precisely in Time.

These people are fascinating and intriguing, even without resorting to end-of-the-world 'prophecies'. I wrote my book mainly to celebrate them.[9] The idea that the Maya calendar (and perhaps the world itself) came to an end in 2012 springs from a single peculiarity: Its 'zero date' (often called the *Era Date*) is not zero. The linear Maya *Long Count* calendar consists of a five-digit date in base-twenty; we modern epigraphers separate the digits by periods: 9.17.10.0.0 or 9.9.2.4.8, for example. The 'Creation' or Era Date is 13.0.0.0.0, and, like a clock after midnight, the next day would have been written either 13.0.0.0.1 or 0.0.0.0.1.[10] The 13.0.0.0.0 'Great Cycle' (this is a modern concept) is a very long time: about 5125 years.

The Maya always accompanied their Long Count dates with the coincident *Tzolk'in* and *Haab* dates (and often several other cycles). The full statement of the Era Date is 13.0.0.0.0, 4 *Ajaw* 8 *Kumk'u*, and when the Maya wished to abbreviate this expression, they called it simply '4 *Ajaw* 8 *Kumk'u*,' or sometimes only '4 *Ajaw*'. We Americans employ a similar honorific abbreviation when we refer to a day in 2001 simply as '9/11'. Though an eleventh day of September arrives every year, to an entire generation those numerals will signify a very specific event. Also, except for a very few, very early dates, a Long Count always includes glyphs for the units (usually called *Bak'tun*, *K'atun*, *Tun*, *Winal*, and Day[11]), not just the five digits. The translation of a Maya Long Count date would look like '...9 *Bak'tuns*, 17 *K'atuns*, 10 *Tuns*, Zero *Winals*, and Zero Days, 12 *Ajaw* 8 *Pax*', for example. The '4 *Ajaw* 8 *Kumk'u*', or '12 *Ajaw* 8 *Pax*', are the *Tzolk'in* and *Haab*, which together we call the *Calendar Round* or **CR**. In fact, the Ancient Maya left us far more dates expressed as CR's than as Long Counts.[12]

Okay, enough of the workings of the Maya calendars! Since

the Era Day in 3114 BC, the Long Count has added up almost thirteen more *Bak'tuns*. At this writing, we passed the *Tun*-ending 12.19.17.0.0 on Wednesday, January 6, 2010; the CR of this date was 3 *Ajaw* 18 *K'ank'in*. This is just three *tuns* before we arrive at the Long Count 13.0.0.0.0 again, on December 21, 2012 (with a CR of 4 *Ajaw* 3 *K'ank'in*)[13]. The End is near! Maybe...

Maya Evidence

Thus, the modern supposition that 2012 is the 'end of the Maya calendar' rests solely on the coincidence of these two LC dates. Elsewhere[14], I have examined every surviving Maya text which refers to 13.0.0.0.0 , either the original in 3114 BC or the 2012 AD repetition. Unfortunately, this data is very scanty. For example, the Era Date in 3114 BC implies that the Maya believed in a *previous* Creation, 5125 years *before* 3114 BC, in 8239 BC. And perhaps others yet earlier, in multiples of five millennia. So far, we have not yet discovered a *single* mention of these purported earlier Creation dates. In Classic Maya texts, we have found reference to many, very ancient events, all expressed in terms of very large intervals and CR dates. None of these include a Long Count, so we have no idea how the Maya would have written it. This is frustrating; we just cannot say yet what the Ancient Maya believed about this issue—or hundreds of others. The main problem with *any* idea we might investigate about them is lack of data. Far more information has been lost than still exists, far more.

We do know something of their mathematics, mainly derived from calendrical calculations and numerology, and what we know of their sophisticated astronomy seems to have been inextricably interwoven with astrology. Our knowledge of their history is basically restricted to what they chose to record in stone,[15] which, as the Reader might imagine, is extremely abbreviated and prejudiced.

Now, what the Maya themselves believed about the 'end' of

their 'Great Cycle' we can only infer from a couple of scattered 'prophecies' and references to the future. These fall into two categories:

(1) Post-Conquest documents, written in Mayan in European letters, from the sixteenth to eighteenth centuries. These include texts such as the *Popol Vuh*, the several *Chilam Balam* books, the *Ritual of the Bacabs*, and ethnographic texts recorded in modern times.

(2) Maya inscriptions from the Classic Period (ca. 300 – 900 AD). A few of these describe events around the Era Date, some mention the future, and one—just one—specifies the date 13.0.0.0.0 4 *Ajaw* 3 *K'ank'in* (21 December 2012, *Tortuguero Monument 6*, featured on the cover of my book[16]). We'll examine this in a moment.

(1) Post-Conquest Documents

The *Popol Vuh*, copied ca. 1700 from a document probably written in the mid-sixteenth century, contains the most complete original Maya Creation myth surviving. It describes the previous three Creations, and a fascinating account of the exploits of the Hero Twins, in the murky limbo preparing for the present Creation. Uncharacteristically, and unexpectedly, it contains *no* dates. Perhaps the Christian Colonial-era target audience for the *Popol Vuh* would have found calendar dates in the Maya system irrelevant or offensive. In any case, although the book contains no prophecies, it does suggest that the Maya may have believed that this cycle was destined to end as well (though it actually is silent on the subject), and—who knows?— the next iteration *might* begin on 13.0.0.0.0.

The *Chilam Balam* books are a group of related texts copied in remote Maya towns from the sixteenth to the nineteenth centuries. *Chilam Balam* means 'Interpreter Jaguar', presumably a title carried by a Maya religious leader. However, the text and imagery of these books contain many references to Christian symbols and beliefs. To an even greater degree than the *Popol Vuh*, they are the result of multiple instances of syncretism, including Nahuatl-Maya and Christian-Maya blendings. Some of these books contain '*Katun* prophecies', a list of thirteen sets of predictions expected to happen in future *k'atuns* (which, the Reader will recall, are approximately twenty-year periods).[17] The 2012 date is 13.0.0.0.0 4 *Ajaw* 3 *K'ank'in*, and the twenty-year period between 1992 and 2012 is *K'atun 4 Ajaw*. Here is what the Prophet tells us to expect:

> The *Quetzal* shall come, the green bird shall come. *Aj K'ante'nal* shall come. Blood-vomit shall come. *K'uk'ulkan* shall come a second time. The Word of God. The *Itza* shall come. (*Chilam Balam of Chumayel*, p. 53, spelling modernized)

A little explanation is in order:

> A *quetzal* is a small, lovely, red-breasted green bird with extraordinary long tail feathers, which resemble leaves of a maize (corn) stalk. It is sacred to the Maya, and is the national bird of Guatemala.

> The Aztec (Nahuatl) word *quetzal* means 'feather'; its Mayan name (also meaning 'feather') is *K'uk'*. *K'uk'ulkan* is the Mayan translation of *Quetzalcoatl* (Nahuatl for 'Feathered Serpent').

> *Aj K'ante'nal* means 'He of the Yellow-Tree Place', or perhaps 'He the Maize-Stalk kernel', a rarely mentioned deity. *K'an* means 'yellow', 'precious' or 'maize'; *K'an-Te'* 'cornstalk' (literally 'maize-tree'). *Nal* means 'place', 'pool,' or 'kernel' (of maize). This character seems to have been a minor god of maize or fertility.

'Blood-vomit' describes one of many Old-World plagues that devastated New World peoples; it had swept through Yucatán just after 1492, during an earlier K'atun 4 Ajaw (a date designation that recurs at regular intervals of 256 years).

K'uk'ulkan was an eponymously named legendary noble ruler, a little like our King Arthur. According to Aztec legend, he promised to return in the (Aztec) year two-Reed, the next one of which will be 2027.

The Itzá were a Maya people, the founders of Chichén Itzá.

I should mention that, despite the blood-vomit, these predictions are actually better than most. Of the thirteen k'atun-prophecies in the Chilam Balam, eight are dire (earthquakes, drought, pestilence, evil rulers, etc.), two are noncommittal, and, counting the one quoted above, only three are good. (See Appendix 1.)

I also hasten to mention that the Chilam Balam books are full of errors and inconsistencies. Dates are wrong, names are misspelled, and even the numbering of the K'atun-prophecies is irregular. Far from the centers of Spanish power and influence, the isolated Maya villages that preserved these traditions were also poor, neglected, and often exploited. Considering how scanty were the surplus resources they had to support their transmission, these weaknesses are forgivable. Indeed, it is remarkable that they were able to preserve any vestiges of Maya history and myth at all. Doubtless far more have been utterly lost.

The Popol Vuh's four Creations are echoed in the Aztec Leyenda de los Soles, 'Legend of the Creations.'[18] This account is much more expansive and specific than the Popol Vuh. It provides more complete descriptions of the lost peoples and the gods which ruled each Cycle. Both the Popol Vuh and the Leyenda *de los Soles* specify the food eaten by each people, and their respective fates. Most importantly, the *Leyenda* provides the beginning and ending dates of each Sun, and even correlates it with the Spanish Calendar.

Despite important differences, it is clear that these two accounts spring from the same source. Presumably, the Aztec copied (and perhaps embellished) an older Maya story. The Aztecs arrived several centuries after the Maya Classic period, and always referred to the East as *In Tlilli in Tlapalli*, land of 'the Red and the Black', that is, the colors of ink, of Books: Land of Wisdom. Caution, however: the *Leyenda de los Soles* was copied 150 years earlier than our copy of the *Popol Vuh* (though the latter's source must date back at least to the same time); the *Popol Vuh* may just have co-opted Aztec myth, and not the other way around.

At present, I still incline to believe that the Maya myth predates the Aztec. This is partly because the Maya describe only four Creations, and the Aztecs, five. I think the extra Creation in the later Aztec account reflects the Maya Collapse, a devastating ecological cataclysm (circa 900 AD)[19] marked by the wholesale abandonment of nearly every great lowland Maya city. The Aztecs simply incorporated this event into the narrative they had inherited, composed during the Maya's glory days preceding the Collapse. 900 AD was only the latest of several Collapses. Similar catastrophes marked the transition between the Preclassic and the Classic (circa 250 AD), as well as the earlier decline of the Olmec (end of the Middle Preclassic, ca. 300 BC) and even earlier, between the Early and Middle Preclassic (ca. 900 BC). Each of these events emptied cities; Mesoamerica is full of ruins. I argue that the multiple Creations in Maya and Aztec myth reflect these multiple Collapses.

(2) Classic-era Documents

Some Maya *stelae* (carved standing-stones) compare a specific

Creation incident to house building. (This event, 'Setting the Hearth' or 'Planting the Three Stones', also reflects the Cosmos.[20] The first order of business in building houses is making a place to cook: traditionally, and most simply, a hole scooped out of the earth for a fire, surrounded by three stones on which one places a griddle to cook tamales or whatever.) I think it is no accident that the Maya verb describing the setting of this tripod (*Tz'apaj*, 'planted') is the same word they use to describe the erection of stelae themselves. In other words, both building a house and planting a stela reenacted a moment of Creation.

Other ancient texts describe 13.0.0.0.0 4 *Ajaw* 8 *Kumk'u* with verbs like 'changed over', 'put in order', and similar expressions. Combined with the *Popol Vuh* Creation stories, we have a tiny fragment of what must have been a much longer and more complex story, rather as if all we had of *Genesis* was ten or twelve sentences. But even if we had a much more complete story, understanding Maya notions of the *last* 13.0.0.0.0 may have little to do with what they expected for the *next* one.

Which is why the mid-seventh-century *Tortuguero Monument 6* is so important. The ancient city of Tortuguero, in southeastern Tabasco, México, has been destroyed, almost completely, by heedless capitalism: a cement plant mined away the hill on which it was built. One of its structures carried a long and beautiful hieroglyphic inscription on three stone plaques arranged in a T-shape. The left arm is lost, and its large middle panel recounts a number of conquests and other events marking the career of its kings. What interests us is the final passage, the last twelve glyphs on the right arm of the T. It counts three *Bak'tuns*, eight *K'atuns*, three *Tuns*, nine *Winals* and two days[21] forward to the 'end of thirteen *Bak'tuns* on 4 *Ajaw* 3 *K'ank'in.*' You can spot the four-dots and three-dots coefficients in the middle of the right two columns. Unfortunately, by some perverse epigraphical Murphy's Law, two of the three most important glyphs—describing the action—are broken away. Better decipherers than I translate the event as:

It will be the end of the 13th *Bak'tun*. It will happen, the witnessing of the display of *Bolon-Yokte'* in the great impersonation.

This is actually much more than we should expect. Several Maya monumental texts look into the future, and the events 'prophesied' are almost always trivial: 'It will be a Thursday, and Lord So-and-So's anniversary.' *Tortuguero Mon. 6* further informs us that a minor deity[22] will dress up, perhaps impersonating a more important god, and that a host will be there to witness the ceremony. This kind of ceremony is par for the course on a *Period-Ending*, that is, a landmark date ending in a string of zeroes. Like our Y2K and decade-endings, a *Period-Ending* (or *PE*) provided an important anchor for historical accounts, and was an occasion for ritual refurbishment of temples, houses, etc. For the most part, major Maya cities erected monuments to mark PEs (usually every five years, or at least every twenty), coronations, and other major ceremonies.

But *Tortuguero Mon. 6* says *nothing* that indicates an 'end' to a calendar cycle or to the world as we know it. It does *not* suggest a transformation of any sort, as far as I can see. The most we can say is that in other contexts, *Bolon Yokte'* was present at the last Creation (on 4 *Ajaw* 8 *Kumk'u*) and seems to be a god of change and perhaps destruction. But his position seems more comparable to the Catholic Saints like St. Lucy (whose province is eyesight and light) or St. Jude (patron of lost causes), whose power is definitely limited.

More importantly, the Palenque text (as well as several other monuments) strongly implies that the ancient Maya did *not* expect the Long Count Calendar to 'reset' after 2012. The Palenque priests, at least, expected the 13.0.0.0.0 Bak'tun to be followed by 14.0.0.0.0, and then 15.0.0.0.0, on up to 19.0.0.0.0.

Then the next big Period Ending in 4774 AD would click over to six digits, that is, 1.0.0.0.0.0, kind of like when your car's odometer reaches 100,000 miles. And what great event did they link to this important date? The eighty-CR anniversary of the coronation of their beloved king, Pakal, eight days later, on 1.0.0.0.0.8 5 *Lamat* 1 *Mol*. That is, the Palenque Maya seem to have expected people in the forty-eighth century to still be celebrating their king's royal jubilee. This certainly implies that they expected no major shifts in consciousness, life, or in the status quo.

In fact, close examination of all the ancient and Colonial period Maya prophetic and Creation texts consistently support the same conclusion: They all expected life to go on just as it was, forever. No change in 2012, or at any time. There is not a single mention of a future cataclysm, collapse, or even a change in the weather, predating Christian influence. They also failed to predict the arrival of the Conquistadors, by far the most devastating event in American History.

Maybe *some* prophets foresaw it, but got as much attention as those decrying the overcutting of their forests! The Maya were no different from any people who are lucky enough to be ascendant: we twenty-first-century Americans (or nineteenth-century British, or second-century Romans, or T'ang-Dynasty Chinese, or twelfth-century Khmers) seem to believe that we are successful because God willed it, and we shall remain ascendant forever. *Revelation* aside, most Americans behave as if the Second Coming is not going to occur any time soon. Everyone has difficulty conceiving of their own mortality, especially nations.

I also hasten to remind you that the Maya lived in dozens of city-states, as different from one another as Athens and Sparta. Despite using the same language and alphabet, and worshipping the same gods, these two cities had extraordinarily different cultures, and their mythologies differed on certain very important issues. No doubt there existed the same kind of diversity among various Maya schools of philosophy and calendrics. Perhaps some groups, like Jehovah's Witnesses, expected an End-of-Times in 2012, or perhaps sooner.[23] And others were doubtless more phlegmatic and/or practical, like the Christian bankers in Florence[24], who hardly ever worried about Armageddon.

In sum, from what the Maya actually tell us—keeping in mind that what we know is but the tiniest *splinter* compared to what we have lost—they apparently expected no change in 2012, but rather that their way of life would continue far into the future. When you hear about 'Mayan Prophecies' and the 'End of the Calendar' (especially if it involves massive Transformation or Destruction), you are really witnessing a massive projection of someone's modern fantasies—fantasies which are being increasingly adopted by some modern Maya religious leaders. Many, many people *hope* that the world will change, and they cling to this date, expecting perhaps, finally, to get their wish. I, for one, believe that we are responsible for our own futures, and if we want Transformation, we are going to have to roll up our sleeves and get to work.

See you in 2013!

Appendix I: A List of the Prophecies of Chilam Balam

From the translation by **Ralph L. Roys,** *The Book of Chilam Balam of Chumayel,* Carnegie Institution of Washington, Publ. 438, Nov. 1933. Mike Coe (personal communication, 2008) warns us:

> If you're using the Ralph Roys translations for the *Chilam Balams,* make sure you get a Yucatec expert to go over the passages before you get them into print. He was very good, but not infallible, and there's a lot more known about Colonial Yucatec Mayan now than there was in his day.

1st Katun: K'atun 11 Ajaw:

...sufficient poison and also ropes to hang their lords ... Niggard is the *katun*, scanty are its rains. ...a *katun* of misery, of importunity (*u tza cizin*) of the devil... **(Bad)**

2nd Katun: K'atun 9 Ajaw:

...The heavenly staff, the heavenly fan (of authority?). The cord descended, the word of God, which came from on high all over the entire world. Nine was its plate, nine was its cup. Make ready, Itzá (for) guests. You shall give them food to eat, and they shall also give you food to eat when they come. **(Noncommittal)**

3rd Katun: K'atun 7 Ajaw:

...lewdness of the wise men, the beckoning of carnal sin... The head-chiefs of the towns, the rulers of the towns, the prophets of the towns, the priests of the Maya men are hanged. Understanding is lost, wisdom is lost. **(Bad)**

4th Katun: K'atun 5 Ajaw:

...Harsh is its face, harsh its tidings, to the ruler. There is affliction... **(Bad)**

5th Katun: K'atun 3 Ajaw:

...fighting; there is a year of locusts. The diminished remainder of the population is hanged ... **(Bad)**

6th (or 1st) Katun: K'atun 1 Ajaw:

...the destroyer of food...seven years the affliction of 8000 warts, for seven years there is the affliction of (invaders?). Then the justice of the Lord, God, shall descend upon carnal sin, upon the worthless rabble of the town, upon the lewd rogue, the rascal. After that there shall come another word, another teaching, but the Maya men shall not admit it to their hearts. **(Very Bad)**

7th (or 2nd) Katun: K'atun 12 Ajaw:

...great artisan, wise man shall come. ... a rich year; there is also an accumulation of wealth. The rains are good ones; the fruit will form. Then they come from the rocks to Christianity ... There shall be neither fox nor kinkajou that will bite. ... This shall be the end of carnal sin... **(Good)**

8th (or 3rd) Katun: K'atun 10 Ajaw:

The hoof shall burn, the sand by the seashore shall burn, the bird's nest shall burn; drought is the charge of the katun... **(Bad)**

9th (or 4th) Katun: K'atun 8 Ajaw:

...The heads of the foreigners to the land were cemented <into the wall (*pak*)> at Chakanputun. (Thompson p. 182)
There is an end to greed, there is an end to causing vexation ... much fighting. **(Good)**

10th (or 4th) Katun: K'atun 6 Ajaw:

Shameless is his speech, shameless his face to the rulers. They shall be the inventors of lewd speech, and then God the Father shall descend to cut their throats because of their sins... **(Bad)**

11th (or 5th) Katun: K'atun 4 Ajaw:

The quetzal shall come, the green bird shall come. *Ah Kantenal* shall come. Blood-vomit shall come (as it did in the last Katun 4 Ahau, the *katun* just before the Conquest). *Kukulcan* shall come with them for a second time. The word of God. The Itza shall come. **(Good)**

12th (or 6th) Katun: K'atun 2 Ajaw:

For half <the katun> there will be bread, for half <the katun> there will be water. The word of God. For half of it there will be a temple for the rulers. (*or:* Its bread, water, and temple are halved.) The end of the word of God. **(Noncommittal)**

13th (or 7th) Katun: K'atun 13 Ajaw:

...judgment (*juicio*) ... Blood shall descend from the tree and the stone. Heaven and earth shall burn ... There shall be no strength in heaven and earth ... There is no lucky day for us ... death from bad blood... **(Bad)**

End Notes

1   Though the process has been going on for over a century, the decipherment of Maya hieroglyphs really did not yield solid readings until about the 1980s.

2   Our 'A.D.' counts the years since the birth of Jesus, a transformative event in Christian history. The Maya Long Count numbers the days since their mythical Creation event on 11 (or 13) August, 3114 BC (Gregorian).

3   In addition, the Maya also fixed events with other calendars: a very precise Lunar day-cycle, a nine-day cycle called 'Lords of the Night', an eighteenth-month cycle of named Moons, an '819-day count' (7x9x13), and other, more arcane cycles.

4   Wednesday is named after the Norse god *Woden* or *Odin*, god of woe (among other qualities). *Thor's* day, the day named in Latin countries for Jupiter, is associated with lightning. I find it fascinating that so many modern people honor, with their day-names, gods they have not worshipped for many centuries.

5   Roman, Greek, and Hebrew numbers, based on letters of the alphabet, become increasingly cumbersome for counting above 1000.

6   *2012: Science and Prophecy of the Ancient Maya*, available at Amazon or at markvanstone.com

7   We don't know which. Maya monuments sometimes refer to ancient dates, usually the 13.0.0.0.0 Era Date and mythic events surrounding it. These just-pre- and just-post-Creation events carry dates like 12.19.13.3.0 (Palenque *Tablet*

of the Cross), and 1.18.5.3.6 (Palenque *Tablet of the Sun*). Unfortunately, we have not found a Long Count date during the first *Bak'tun* (400-year period, more correctly *Pik*), so we don't know yet whether Maya scribes would have written such a date, say, 0.3.14.6.16 or 13.3.14.6.16. Probably either, depending on the context, just as we do. Most of us say thirty minutes after midnight is 12:30, but in military situations, this time is 0:30. My digital watch gives me both options. There was much diversity of expression between Maya cities, and I expect that some scribes preferred to write it one way, and others the other way. All surviving (contemporaneous) Long Counts lie between 7.16.0.0.0 and 10.4.0.0.0 (About 40 BC – 908 AD); apparently the LC calendar was in use for somewhere above 1000 years.

8   Each unit is twenty times the following (except the *Tun*, which is eighteen *Winals*). A *Tun* is approximately a year, with 360 (=18 x 20) days, and a *K'atun* (actually called *Winikhaab*) is about twenty years. The *Bak'tun* (we know now it was actually called *Pik*) is twenty *K'atuns*/400 *Tuns*, equaling about 394 years. We call base-twenty numbers *vigesimal*, and base-ten numbers *decimal*: Our decimal date 2013 works the same way, except the units are all ten times the preceding: **3** years, + (**1** x 10 years), + (**0** x 100 years), + (**2** x 1000 years). Many scholars, to be consistent, use the Mayan word for 'day' or 'sun', *K'in*, instead of the English word *Day*.

9   A CR date, always consisting of a *Tzolk'in* followed by a *Haab*, is a unique day in a *CR cycle*, thirteen days short of 52 years. A date such as 4 *Ajaw* 8 *Kumk'u* would occur every 52 years, and most people would witness only one such date in their lifetimes. For this reason, most Maya inscriptions found it sufficient to express dates in, say, a certain king's reign, with the CR only.

10   Some scholars calculate a slightly different correlation

between the Maya and Christian calendars. The one I am using is called *Goodman-Martinez-Thompson* (GMT), named for its primary discoverers/calculators. Many scholars, including my friend and co-author Michael D. Coe, prefer *GMT+2*, which places the 13.0.0.0.0 date two days later, on December 23rd, 2012.

11 That is, in my book, *2012: Science and Prophecy of the Ancient Maya*. I also submitted an article for a collection edited by Joseph Gelfer, *2012: Decoding the Countercultural Apocalypse*. (Both published in 2010.) You may also access my websubsite http://www.famsi.org/research/vanstone/2012/index.html , or my blog at http://2012science.wordpress.com/ .

12 Some skeletal chronicles also survive in late-colonial Maya documents like the *Chilam Balam of Chumayel*.

13 *2012: Science and Prophecy of the Ancient Maya*. See note 11.

14 *K'atuns* are named for their final *Tzolk'in* day. Due to calendrical mathematics, there are only thirteen choices: 1 *Ajaw*, 2 *Ajaw*, ... up to 12 *Ajaw*, and 13 *Ajaw* (...not in that order, however: 5 *Ajaw* is followed by 3 *Ajaw*, then 1 *Ajaw*, then 12 *Ajaw*, ... ending in 7 *Ajaw*). The full cycle of thirteen *k'atuns* comprises approximately 256 years, so the *K'atun* Prophecy for 2012 also applied to the years 1736-1756, and 1480-1500, and 1224-1244, and on back.

15 Aztecs called each Creation Cycle a 'Sun', as each began and ended on a certain calendar day. The center of the Aztec 'Calendar Stone' portrays the head of *Tonatiuh*, the Sun God.

16 Much debate and spilled ink surrounds this 'mysterious' event. What we know is that the surprisingly large and rapidly growing Maya population suddenly (over a period of about fifty years) abandoned most of their glorious cities to the encroaching jungle. During the last, turbulent years, these cities also suffered increased warfare, perhaps

fighting over diminished provisions. It was probably worse than the Black Plague in fourteenth-century Europe; maybe half the population—or more—died. I think that, whatever associated disasters exacerbated the Collapse, it primarily resulted from the Maya's overexploitation of their forest resources, pushing the land beyond a healthy carrying capacity. A few years of drought and resulting crop failures caused widespread famine; desperate populations migrated far away from their cities, and never returned. The ecology of Europe is much more resilient than that of Mesoamerica, and of the Maya jungle in particular. When the latter fell, they fell hard. No doubt there were Maya Cassandras—the equivalent of today's Sierra Club and Greenpeace—striving to divert their greedy and foolish leaders from their self-destructive course. Apparently, the leaders heeded those ancient alarmists as carefully as our leaders do today. The end really *is* near!

17 For a comprehensive (if slightly out-of-date) account of this mythology, see Linda Schele, David Friedel, and Joy Parker, *Maya Cosmos*, New York 1993. Also see Karen Bassie-Sweet, *Maya Sacred Geography and the Creator Deities*, Oklahoma, 2008.

18 3.8.3.9.2 is 490,862 days, or almost 1344 years. Counted from the contemporaneous events recorded here in 668 AD, this reaches December 21st, 2012 AD.

19 *Bolon Yokte'* means something like '9-Root Tree' or 'Many are his Supports' ('9' to the Maya also means 'lots'). This deity (it sometimes carries the epithet -*K'uh*, 'god' or 'gods') might be 'they': it *might* represent nine gods, or even a larger crowd. Many Maya gods had multiple personalities.

20 I should mention that the Aztec *Leyenda de los Soles* tells us that this 'Sun'/Creation began (and will end) on a 4-Movement day. It states that the end will take the form of a mighty earthquake. It also firmly implies that this 'Sun' will

probably last no longer than 13 Calendar Rounds (676 years), precisely, at a time when we stop feeding the gods with blood-sacrifices. Now, my calculations suggest that the probable begin-date for this 'Sun' was 1195 (give or take 52 years), in which case the world should have ended in 1871 (give or take 52 years). Perhaps our wars and automobile accidents are providing enough blood to satisfy the thirsty gods. It's ironic to think that, should we achieve world peace and better automobile airbags, the Aztec gods would reward our efforts with the End of the World.

21 It was they who first decided that God did not really hate usurers, and started charging interest on their loans, a decision that funded the early Renaissance.

Chapter Seven

Creating the Intention for the Unity Consciousness of the Ninth Wave of the Mayan Calendar

Carl Johan Calleman

In recent years there has been radically increased interest in the Mayan calendar, especially its end, and so many ask what this tells us about the future. Surprisingly, many people ask this question as if the answer had nothing to do with themselves or the choices they make. Few seem to have considered that the fulfillment of the cosmic plan will require of them to step up to the role of co-creators with this divine plan. This is not to say that human beings can just create anything they want at any point in time. The waves of consciousness brought by the Mayan calendar still define the framework of our existence and what we may or may not be able to create in any given era. Yet, only the creativity that is consistent with a new wave will be favored and this will again be evident as we enter the ninth, and highest, wave of the Mayan calendar system. It is thus pertinent to ask what consciousness the ninth wave will create and what it will require of us to be able to step up to becoming co-creators with this wave.

To address this we need to consult the ancient Maya and look at their only inscription, which describes the meaning of the end of their calendar, the Tortuguero Monument 6. This says that at that point in time the nine-step entity, Bolon Yookte, will 'descend'.[1] In layman's terms, this means that a combination of nine cosmic forces, nine wave movements, will simultaneously manifest fully. In this ancient Mayan way of looking at the meaning of the end of the calendar, *there is thus nothing that speaks of an end to the world.* Rather, what the end of the calendar system is all about is a completion, or fulfillment, of evolutionary processes that have been going on from the beginning of time and led the world to what it is today.

These nine cosmic forces are the nine evolutionary progressions (Underworlds), each through thirteen energies from which the prophetic Mayan calendar system is made, a system which significant events in biological and historical evolution correlate extremely well with. The different progressions each develop a different frame of consciousness and currently we are most strongly influenced by the eighth wave. It is, however, the ninth and highest of these wave movements that will bring about the final shift to unity consciousness that will culminate as the calendar comes to an end. I feel it is imperative to realize that these nine cosmic forces are not acting separately from the human beings, but through their influence on us and so they will only manifest inasmuch as the humans align with them. I feel we also need to consider that the co-creation of this highest level requires that we are truly committed to its purpose. It is in preparation of this somewhat mysterious wave that I encouraged the celebration of the Conscious Convergence, July 17-18, 2010, as a point to focus on aligning with the highest and decisive wave of the Mayan calendar system, the ninth wave.

Many people have an intuitive sense that the end of the Mayan calendar will bring a shift in consciousness. Yet, the source of such a shift is rarely clearly stated or explained exactly how it will happen or what would be its nature. Maybe, however, shifts in consciousness are actually a little less mysterious than many people tend to believe. In fact, shifts in consciousness have been happening from the beginning of time and continue to happen whenever there is a significant energy shift in the Mayan calendar, such as between any of its *days* and *nights*.

Despite all these previous shifts in cosmic history, I feel that there is something very special and significant about the new consciousness that may be expected to be generated by the ninth wave. To begin with, for all that we know, it is designed to bring *a shift to unity consciousness* where the human mind will no longer be dominated by any dark filter. We will, in other words, become 'transparent', and I believe this is the particular consciousness—seeing reality the way it is with no separation—that so many are waiting for. This is not just any consciousness, but one that transcends the dualities of the past and aids the human being to see the unity of all things. The reason that this kind of unity consciousness can be beneficial to the planet, and to mankind, is that it is one that leads to the transcendence of all separation (between man and woman, man and nature, ruler and ruled, east and west, etc). I feel that without the manifestation of such a shift in consciousness, the world will sooner or later come to an end. People with a dualist and separating consciousness are somewhat like cancer cells in the body of the Earth, with little regard to its larger whole, and would eventually generate a collapse of its ecosystem. Only a shift to unity consciousness will forever stop the unchecked exploitation of the Earth and, on a deeper level, make us understand that we are part of creation and need to live in harmony with it. But will such a shift just happen automatically?

As mentioned above, global consciousness shifts have their origin in the resonance with the cosmic forces described by the Mayan calendar. Hence, even though some may temporarily have experienced altered states of consciousness, it is only in as much as a shift is induced in accordance with the cosmic plan. As we may understand from the Mayan calendar, this will be here to stay. Thus, only with the ninth wave may a shift to unity consciousness be regarded as something whose time has truly come. This is the wave that will cap off all previous evolution of mankind and build the bridge that will allow us to enter the new world that will follow upon the end of the calendar.

On the other hand, the student of the Mayan calendar will know that, in order for a consciousness shift to manifest, human beings must be in resonance with it and, at some point at least, have subconsciously made a choice to align with it. Hence, a large-scale consciousness shift is not something that can happen against the will of the human beings. Especially at the highest levels of evolution, such as the ninth, it can only happen through human beings that choose to serve as co-creators. Unfortunately, many have been led to believe that there is some physical event to wait for, such as a pole shift, Nibiru, sun flares, or a galactic alignment, resulting in a passive attitude that has made the Mayan calendar seem disempowering and events as being outside of their power to influence. I believe, however, that, as the Hopi are saying, 'We are the ones that we have been waiting for'. *If we make the commitment to do so, we can co-create unity consciousness with the ninth wave.*

As many readers of this book may have experienced, there are spiritual practices, healing techniques and methods for personal development that, in fact, do cause temporary shifts in consciousness and the experience of unity of all things. Yet, what seems to be missing for such transformations to play a positive role on a larger scale is the *commitment* of a critical mass of people to create a world based on such unity consciousness. The idea behind the Conscious Convergence, July 17-18, 2010, was thus to create a powerful intention to do so. There is, in fact, one thing that is always in our power to do — and in the power of all human beings to do — and this is to *intend* to create and manifest unity consciousness. As the student of the law of attraction will know, all manifestation begins with an intention and without an intention there is no result. *The Conscious Convergence — A Wave of Unity is thus for all those who intend to manifest unity consciousness.* (It may be important to point out that it is not about intending any shift of consciousness, but one to *unity* consciousness). It is for those who authentically will say: 'I intend to manifest unity consciousness'. Whatever you believe in, whatever worldview you have, it is still in your power to intend such a shift for yourself and others. The proposed dates were timely for setting the intention to do so in that they lead up to a manifestation of unity consciousness during the ninth wave, in alignment with the cosmic plan. Without such a widespread intention, it is doubtful whether there will ever be such a shift on this planet, either individually or collectively.

Based on the creation of such an intention in the Conscious Convergence, it seems natural that people will also want to perform ceremonies and participate in spiritual practices that are manifestations of such a unity consciousness, and seek whatever ways are possible to make permanent its results. In fact is that *the Conscious Convergence should be looked upon as the beginning of a process toward deepened unity consciousness that never stops.* This is the kind of commitment that I believe will be required. For those desiring to fulfill the cosmic plan, the Conscious Convergence should be an entry point to co-creating the ninth wave and something we should never want to drop out of. To start following the Mayan calendar on a daily basis from this point *within the framework provided by the Ninth wave* may, in fact, by itself be a significant factor for developing unity consciousness. Only with deadlines do projects become real, and the calendar provides us with a time frame within which this is to be accomplished.

It seems important that manifestations linked to the Conscious Convergence are planned very carefully and express this new unity consciousness, so that they are not just thoughtlessly applied expressions of the old world we have been living in. If, for instance, artistic performances are part of the celebration, it seems wise to consider whether these are enhancing the experience of unity of all or if they create an experience of separation between the artists and the audience.

The same may apply to the performance of ceremonies if the leader is not truly inclusive. A good example of a ceremony that is an expression of unity consciousness is, in my mind, when Jack Sully in *Avatar* is taken up as a member of the people of Pandora. Furthermore, if for the generation of unity consciousness valuable spiritual practices are used, it is important to consider whether irrelevant worship of founders or gurus can be excluded. Maybe silent and low key common practices are, in fact, the most powerful manifestations of unity consciousness, but regardless, it is important that participants walk their talk and do not recreate dominance structures. How to do this would be for local organizers to decide; here, it is only the importance of approaching this issue with fresh eyes and attention to detail that is emphasized.

The name Conscious Convergence alludes to the Harmonic Convergence, a mind-opening gathering on August 17-18, 1987 (1 Imix and 2 Ik) and so it is important to point out the relationship between the two and why, after so many years, there is a second one, July 17-18, 2010 (13 Eb and 1 Ben)[2]. The important commonality between the two Convergences is that they both are (essentially) placed in time at a doubling of the eighth and ninth wave movements of the Mayan calendar. Hence, they reflect energy shifts that herald the respective trans-formations of consciousness brought by these waves. Put in other terms, *what the Harmonic Convergence meant to the quantum jump to the eighth wave, the Conscious Convergence will mean to the quantum jump to the ninth wave.*[3] (It can be understood as a second Harmonic Convergence). Or, if we include the seventh wave and its pre-wave for comparison, we may see that it will mean to the preparation for the ninth wave what the European Renaissance meant to the quantum jump to the modern world of industrialism. What is different now, and a challenge for the Conscious Convergence, is that this step cannot be said to be in the interest of separate individuals, but rather of all of humanity.

From these parallels, we may see that the Conscious Convergence by itself is not the beginning of the ninth wave, which does not start until March 9, 2011.[4] Rather, *this celebration initiates a wave, a pre-wave, which precedes and paves the ground for the ninth wave* and directly leads into it. The Conscious Convergence is thus tremendously important as a point for creating the intention of unity consciousness, even if this will only be fully developed later with the ninth wave. Maybe it will, in fact, be humanity's last chance of setting such an intention, which almost with necessity must exist at an early point if we are to elevate ourselves above the economic chaos that we may expect in the years ahead. In my own view, *the hope for the future lies exactly in learning to surf on this ninth wave and so transcending, rather than getting caught up in, all the dualities and conflicts of lower Underworlds.* If this is so, it must also be expected that the Conscious Convergence will meet with much resistance from all those forces that are defending the ego-based operation of the old world and the massive hierarchies this has generated. As a small example of this, a commercial media industry has now emerged around '2012', speculating about what is going to happen, as if this was independent of the intentions and creative direction people choose. Naturally, we will also come to be faced with our own cynicism and apathy towards the state of the world and thoughts will come back to us as: 'This is not possible', 'The world will not change', etc., and it is for this reason that a strong commitment will be needed.

The Conscious Convergence is meant to be a very inclusive event that can be embraced by everyone who intends the emergence of unity consciousness, regardless of his or her views about the Mayan calendar or otherwise. It is about positively and constructively using a window of opportunity, and so participation in this only requires an insight that the consciousness shift must come out of the evolutionary processes of which we are currently a part. Thus, a shift to unity consciousness is not something that will simply drop down on us from the sky at some date in the future, but can only evolve from the point where we are at the present moment. It is a basic tenet of the law of attraction that providence only moves when you are committed. So far, however, the commitment for a transition to unity consciousness has not surfaced on a larger scale or even been proposed previously.

For this event to be successful in generating the intention for the shift to the consciousness of the ninth wave, a massive participation will be desirable from the preparatory stages. The preparatory efforts have to be shared by the millions that intend a shift in consciousness to take place. To bring it about, a collective effort will thus be needed and already making a choice to participate is part of creating the intention that has been discussed here. Initially, there will be a great need for people to take initiatives to disseminate the call for the Conscious Convergence around the world. It is important to approach organizations to have them embrace it. Then there will be the need for people to make their unique contributions known through public websites, social media and other networks. There will also be a need for funding of many aspects of the activities and for staff, which can be done through to www.commonpassion.org, a 501c3 non-profit, public benefit corporation. Then, there will be a need for creative planning of events and the creation of a network between these. Individuals and organizations wishing to participate in this global program are invited to join the discussion for particulars of the shared intention and to connect with others around the world co-creating this intentional wave of unity consciousness. A discussion forum has been initiated at:
http://forum.commonpassion.org/viewforum.php?id=50.

My own view is that this is the last chance that human beings will have to truly align themselves with the cosmic plan. It is now or never, and if you do not think that the Conscious Convergence has something to do with you, you probably have not studied the Mayan calendar seriously enough. Hence, there can be no proxies for your participation in the transformation of the world as the calendar comes to an end. The final descent of Bolon Yookte, the Nine Waves (Nine Lords of Time or Nine Underworlds, or whatever name you prefer) is upon us and it is not without reason that the number nine is sacred in so many spiritual traditions. Nine is the destiny number of humanity, and so it will be your own choice whether you want to be part of co-creating this destiny.

End Notes

1   See for instance my article on the Tortuguero monument: http://www.calleman.com/content/articles/the_tortuguero %20_monument.htm.

2   The Conscious Convergence is not based on tzolkin days, but rather on the fractal time acceleration of the nine waves. Yet, we may still pay attention to the tzolkin day of the event. Thus July 17, 2010 is 13 Eb, one of the more mysterious day signs that is typically translated as The Road or Grass and, since it is linked to the number thirteen, this day is very typical of the Eb day sign. Road usually refers to the road of life or the road up the cosmic pyramid, and grass refers to a grass roots event. Typically, people born in this day sign are those that have the concern for seven generations into the future, do much good, but do not to seek the limelight for themselves.

3   This is not how the Harmonic Convergence was originally understood by Tony Shearer and José Argüelles, who first proposed the dates; they saw the Harmonic Convergence as the end point of Thirteen Heavens, starting AD 843, and the Nine Hells (52-year periods) that had followed upon Hernan Cortez landing in Vera Cruz in 1519. Argüelles promoted

this scheme in *The Mayan Factor*. While this may have
served as a guiding prophecy that intuitively led to identifying the dates of the Harmonic Convergence as August 16-
17, 1987 (1 Alligator and 2 Wind), in my view it hardly
serves as a theoretical understanding of why these dates
were actually energetically important. Thus, the Harmonic
Convergence was defined more mythologically than scientifically, since at the time the knowledge of the reality basis
of the Mayan calendar was almost non-existent. We now
know from Mayan sources that 13+9 is not to be regarded as
a linear sequence, but that *each of the Nine Underworlds was
made up from Thirteen Heavens*. Thus, according to the Mayan
Books of Chilam Balam 'the nine lords of time *(Bolon-ti-ku)
seized* the thirteen lords of time *(Oxlahun-ti-ku)*' and so
creation has an integrated pyramidal rather than linear
structure. Whether people are aware of it or not, the entire
evolution of the cosmos since the Big Bang has also been
meticulously mapped out in light of the Mayan calendar
and verified by massive empirical evidence.

4   I have probably contributed to the confusion that reigns
when it comes to the beginning date of the Universal wave
movement, and have given different times for this. What we
know is that the calendar develops according to nine wave
movements, where the longest one goes back to the birth of
the universe, and they all differ from one another with a
factor of twenty. According to such a fractal view of the
prophetic Mayan calendar system, the ninth wave would
then be only 234 days long made up of thirteen different
uaxaclahunkin (eighteen) periods. This places the
beginning of the ninth wave at March 9, 2011 and that of the
preceding wave (Conscious Convergence) at July 17, 2010.
These are points in time that are expected to mark significant frequency increases and accelerations of time.

As we approach the time when all the nine waves, developing at different speeds, will simultaneously come to manifest fully (28 October 2011, 13 Ahau) there is going to be quite complex overlapping patterns of these waves. The Sacred Calendar rounds of 260 days will still have an unquestionable energetic existence and so these, as part of this overlapping, would continue the three stage rocket into the birth of the new world that started on 9.9.9 (Sept 9, 2009), see http://www.calleman.com/content, (articles/999_and_ the_mayan_calendar.htm). For this reason, the dates of the beginnings of the two next tzolkin rounds, May 27, 2010 and Feb 11, 2011, will also remain as important times for celebrating alignments with the cosmic plan and are potentially very important for the preparation for the Conscious Convergence and the actual ninth wave respectively.

This chapter is from a paper given by Dr. Calleman and subsequently published; thus the sequencing of dates and time references found herein.

Chapter Eight

Conscious Medicine

Gill Edwards

Why are we seeing so much chronic and degenerative disease these days? Why is our health not improving, despite throwing trillions of dollars at it every year? Why does medical treatment cause so many deaths? What is wrong with our healthcare system? Perhaps the problem is that conventional medicine goes into battle with illness and disease. It shoots the messenger— silencing warning signals from the body that something is awry, that energy-consciousness is not flowing freely. It sees the body as stupid, faulty and inadequate. It battles against viruses and bacteria and inflammation and tumors. It views disease as an enemy, which needs to be shot down. Zap it! Cut it out! Radiate it! No questions asked.

Could it be that the paradigm that conventional medicine is built upon is the very worldview that makes us sick—a fear-based, materialist model based on separation from love and oneness? And perhaps the hidden purpose of illness and disease is to push us to expand our consciousness, and shift towards a new paradigm? Could illness be a friend and teacher, rather than an enemy? As Einstein said, you cannot solve a problem from the same level of thinking which caused it.

Imagine a company that makes wooden garden furniture, all of which is painted green. The company is highly successful, and all goes well, until some of the furniture begins to emerge from the factory in bright pink. No one wants to buy it, and the pink furniture begins to pile up outside the gates, causing a blockage for wood and paint supplies coming in, and for green furniture going out. Eventually a consultant is called in, who suggests a solution: they should take on more painting staff and buy in extra green paint, and repaint the pink furniture as it emerges from the factory. However, the repainted green furniture doesn't look as good as the originals, and has to be sold at a lower price. Even worse, more and more of the furniture is now coming out pink, so the problems are growing. So the consultant suggests taking on even more staff, and buying even more green paint.

Now the factory has some new problems: the additional staff is blocking the gates, and profits are reduced by the extra costs and lower selling prices. The company is running into financial difficulties. So the consultant suggests they borrow money from the bank, and take on extra staff in the accounts department. By now, almost all of the furniture is coming out pink; the company has a bank loan to repay each month, and even more staff to pay. They are now heading towards bankruptcy. The consultant's advice covered up the initial problem, but created a whole set of new problems. And still no one has asked *why* the garden furniture is being painted pink, and *who* gave those new instructions.

This is pretty much how conventional medicine operates. If your spleen isn't producing enough insulin, doctors call it diabetes, and prescribe extra insulin on a daily basis. If your blood pressure is too high, you are given drugs that aim to lower it (though these are fairly ineffective and carry considerable health risks). If you have heavy periods or fibroids, you might have your womb removed to 'solve' the problem. If you feel depressed, you are prescribed the latest round of (almost useless) anti-depressants. If you have pain in your knee, a doctor might prescribe painkillers or an anti-inflammatory, or a surgeon might scrape out the area beneath your knee. The problem is given a name—such as diabetes, fibroids, hypertension, depression or osteoarthritis—and the diagnostic label is then seen as the 'explanation' for the problem. You 'have' arthritis, or you 'have' depression, which is rather like calling it Pink Paint Syndrome. Then drugs or surgery are prescribed in an attempt to cover up the pink paint.

From a new paradigm perspective, if you focus on the physical level, and try to solve problems *at that level,* you are not seeing the bigger picture. Any organizational consultant worth his or her salt would go straight to the CEO or top management team, and find out what was *causing* the pink paint problem. Is there a lack of communication? Is there conflict between the managers? Is there a supply problem? Is someone trying to sabotage the company's success? Is there a new vision for the company? What is really going on? Through conflict resolution, healthy communication and clarifying the company's vision, the consultant will not only iron out the problem, but also create a stronger and healthier company for the future. And this is exactly what the emerging new paradigm of conscious medicine aims to do.

The Ghost in the Machine

It sounds pretty obvious to look for the cause of problems, rather than painting over the symptoms—so why doesn't it happen within conventional medicine? It doesn't happen within conventional medicine because its model of reality starts and stops at the physical level. It is blind to the very existence of the CEO and management team. It sees the factory workers as automatons that can develop faults, and need to be corrected. It sees the body as a machine that can wear out, go wrong or have faulty parts. The body is merely a bag of biochemistry and genes, which is somehow disconnected from the *person.*

How did this mysterious state of affairs come about? Well, let's take a brief excursion into history. During the Reformation, when the rational, masculine world of Protestantism suppressed the more feminine world of Catholicism and the Holy Mother, a new science was also born. In the seventeenth century, Newton developed the idea of a 'clockwork universe', which had been set into motion by God, then left to its own devices; Descartes split mind from body, and saw the person as a mere 'ghost in the machine'; and scientists came to an arrangement with the Church whereby science would deal with the visible world (including nature and the body), while religion would address the unseen realms (including the mind and morality).

By the end of the seventeenth century, in the eyes of science, nature was no longer seen as sacred or even as alive. It had merely become inanimate matter in motion. And God was becoming increasingly irrelevant. The Cartesian-Newtonian model of the universe was born.

It was another 300 years before we began to see the problems created by such a mechanistic and fragmented view of reality — a view which not only informs how we currently see reality, but which also became the basis of conventional medicine. Whenever you pop a pill because you have a headache, or see a doctor over recurrent sore throats, who then peers down your throat to see 'what is wrong', you might not be aware that you are seeing the world through the eyes of Newton and Descartes — but you are. The question of who is occupying the sick body is seen as irrelevant. You have become a mere ghost in the machine.

If you were born in an indigenous culture that uses traditional methods of healing, the idea of suppressing symptoms with drugs, or looking more closely at the body to find out what the problem is would be seen as patently absurd. It would be taken for granted that something is out of whack with *you* — with your current relationships with self, others, life or the spirit world — and the focus would be on restoring 'good relations', so that your energy could flow in healthy ways. Traditional healers or shamans might also use herbs or other natural equivalents of modern drugs, but they see symptoms or illness within a bigger picture. They look at the whole person, their context and their environment. They seek to address the cause, not the symptom—and always see disease as an expression of *dis-ease* within the self.

One Native American shaman, when asked by a Western doctor how he would treat arthritis, replied 'I don't know—bring her to me and I'll show you'. He did not treat diseases; he only treated people. He devoted time to hearing the 'story' behind someone's illness, rather than simply rushing to a diagnosis and dispensing treatment mechanically. Once you understand the whole story, there is an opportunity for true *healing*—rather than temporary relief of symptoms. Good doctors still know this. The reassuring bedside manner of the old-fashioned family doctor was far closer to the traditional shaman than to the modern techno-medic who dispenses pills, anxiously arranges batteries of tests, or refers you to a 'specialist' (who has studied a single part of your body in detail, and has an even more fragmented view than a family doctor).

Doctors have been accused of becoming mere pimps for the pharmaceutical industry, and widely satirized for their fragmentary approach to the body, and for seeing patients as 'the appendix in bed 3'. Yet every doctor I know has a strong intention to be a healer, is well aware of the limitations of modern medicine—and is hungry for change.

The Material Universe
It is easy to forget that science simply offers a *story* about reality, rather than the objective truth. Just as religion was once taken to be the whole Truth, scientists and doctors have become the new priests of our age, whose opinions are often taken to be factual and accurate. But our ever-changing science is just a story—and stories are neither true nor false. They are just more or less helpful and enlightening. And it seems that a new story is now unfolding.

The Cartesian-Newtonian worldview is based upon materialism. That is, it sees the world as real and solid, and assumes that the physical world is all there is. In this clockwork universe, everything is made up of separate objects, which can bump up against each other like billiard balls, but which have no real connection. What really matters in this worldview is the solid stuff—the 'matter'—and everything else can be explained at that level.

To the materialist, the body is a machine—and consciousness is a mere epiphenomenon. Mind somehow emerged from the primordial broth and random genetic mutations, presumably because it had some advantage in survival terms as animals slowly evolved from the plant kingdom. But since mind is not 'solid stuff', it is not really important.

Despite overwhelming evidence to the contrary, the materialist assumes that mind cannot affect matter, that consciousness cannot affect anything at a distance, and that mind and matter are fundamentally different 'stuff'. If you see through these blinkered eyes, then drugs and surgery do make sense as an approach to healthcare. If the body is sick, you correct it at the physical level, since the physical level is all there is. You ignore the mind because it is pretty much irrelevant to the physical body. Isaac Newton himself was deeply religious, but a die-hard materialist would now pooh-pooh the very notion of God or any spirituality. To a materialist, if you cannot see and touch it, it isn't real!

Is materialism even a *scientific* basis for healthcare, let alone a helpful approach? Well, it depends upon which century your 'science' comes from! In recent decades, a new model of the universe has been emerging from the cutting edge of science—a model which turns our common-sense reality upside-down and inside-out. Countless scientists and visionaries are saying that our way of seeing reality is in the midst of a stunning transformation. We are collectively shifting from a belief in a material universe—a world of solid stuff—towards an awareness of everything as energy-consciousness.

It might seem like a no-brainer that the world is solid and material. After all, I can see and touch this laptop, cup my hands around this hot mug and taste my peppermint tea. But that is only because we are so good at interpreting complex vibrational frequencies through our senses, and converting them into experiences. The world is not as it appears to be. *Everything is energy, and energy is inseparable from consciousness.*

This is a shift in awareness that is far more profound and significant to our everyday lives than realizing that the earth is round rather than flat. It is a mind-blowing shift, which shatters our old assumptions about how the world works. When you fully absorb what it means, it changes *everything*. And healthcare can never be the same again.

The Paradigm Shift

As a teenager, I was fascinated by research in parapsychology which had produced staggering statistics—studies of telepathy, psycho-kinesis, remote viewing and other psychic phenomena, which have shown that minds can pick up information in non-physical ways, and that mind can affect matter at a distance, with odds of millions or even billions to one against chance. Extensive studies have shown that the mind can affect a random number generator, for example, with odds against chance of more than a *trillion* to one. (To get this into perspective, results are seen as statistically significant in science—for example, a new drug can scrape through a drug trial and be marketed as effective—if the odds against chance are just *twenty* to one!)

I was even more fascinated, as a budding psychologist, as to why scientists would pooh-pooh or deny the implications of such research, and how people could say that they did not 'believe' in telepathy or clairvoyance. It wasn't a scientific viewpoint—it was merely prejudice. It seemed to me like saying they did not believe in Australia, simply because they had not visited it themselves.

The British healer and psychic Matthew Manning was eager, as a young man, to have his extraordinary abilities confirmed by science. He took part in scientific trials for several years, and proved that he could inhibit the growth of cancer cells in a laboratory setting, over and over again. However, he was still met with skepticism, accusations of being a fraud, and the 'need for further trials'. What he did was simply impossible within the old materialist worldview—and he eventually realized that no amount of 'proof' would satisfy the skeptics. He became disillusioned with science, and decided to devote his life to the more productive and satisfying work of healing.

Soon after Matthew Manning became famous as a teenage psychic, I came across Thomas Kuhn's classic book about paradigm shifts on my undergraduate reading list—and began to understand why scientists could be so unscientific. I learnt that there is always huge resistance to seeing the world in a whole new way. This resistance usually begins with patronizing denial, as the new ideas are denounced as 'stuff and nonsense'. Later on, as the new movement gains ground, the 'old guard' moves into aggressive resistance.

Thank heavens people are no longer burnt at the stake for having heretical views—but they can still be thrown out of their jobs, ridiculed, threatened or lose their former status. Heretics are not always popular, and many learnt to keep their mouths shut. (I lived for a while with a theoretical physicist who would never have dared to air his mystical views at work. Back in 1543, Copernicus wisely left his theory to be published posthumously, thirty years after he realized that Earth is *not* at the centre of the solar system.)

Eventually, so much evidence accumulates for a new model that the old paradigm becomes untenable. The earth really *is* round. We *do* revolve around the sun! Telepathy really *does* happen! People *can* heal others with focused intention! We really *do* create our own reality! It becomes more and more obvious, and those who were clinging to the old view retire or die, or simply declare they had known it all along. It is as if the whole world puts on a new pair of spectacles, and now sees reality differently. The new worldview seeps into the collective consciousness, and now begins to be considered normal and common sense — yet society has made a massive change in how the everyday world is seen. A cultural renaissance has occurred, and consciousness has evolved towards seeing a bigger picture.

As I read more and more about the new physics, I came to realize that we were heading toward a paradigm shift — and that instead of matter being seen as primary, we were moving towards seeing consciousness as primary. Having read so much about mysticism as a teenager, this sounded very familiar. As physicist Sir James Jeans put it, 'The universe begins to look more like a great thought than like a great machine.'

As we shall see, if we apply this to healthcare and medicine, it says that, the body begins to look more like a great thought than like a great machine.

And so it does!

The Conscious Universe

Back in the 1920s, quantum physics began to reveal a very different world from that inhabited by the materialist: a world in which mystics, ghosts, telepathy and distant healing could come to co-exist happily alongside computers, jet planes and MRI scans. In the bizarre world of quantum physics, we can move backwards or forwards in time, communication can occur instantaneously across vast distances between 'entangled' particles, and light can be a wave or a particle depending on who is observing it.

What is more, as physicists looked at tinier and tinier particles of what makes up our physical reality, they concluded that there simply isn't any solid stuff. There is only energy, or 'waves of probability'. And what is it that *decides* which of many probable realities comes into existence, so that it appears to be real and solid? Consciousness. The new physics tells us that *consciousness* determines whether light behaves as a wave or a particle, or whether this event or that event occurs. If we take this further, it is consciousness that decides whether this knee is painfully swollen or healthy, or whether this tumor is here or not here.

For example, in my *Conscious Medicine* workshops, I often show a video from China in which a woman with bladder cancer is treated at the Hospital With No Medicine near Beijing. The woman lies down, and a large tumor is clearly visible on an ultrasound screen. Three experienced Qi Gong practitioners then send chi towards the tumor. (Chi is also known as ki, prana, mana, vital force, Source energy or the Holy Spirit.) In just over a minute, the tumor becomes transparent and reduces by half; it then suddenly vanishes as if it were merely a wisp of smoke. The healers decided that the tumor was 'not here', while holding a high state of consciousness—and the tumor promptly obliged by shifting into another probable reality. The healers briefly applaud their own success—but it is clear that it is all in a day's work for them. (A German film crew later captured a tumor dissolving in eleven seconds at the same hospital.)

Crucially, these 'operations' in China are only performed after training the client in Qi Gong for several weeks, so that they are inducted into an energetic worldview, and have an effective tool for maintaining their own energy flow. Without this shift, it is understood that a tumor would simply grow again. At the Hospital With No Medicine, practitioners are aware that the world is made of energy-consciousness—and that a tumor is simply a bundle of condensed energy that can respond to focused intention.

The new physics tells us that energy-consciousness, rather

than 'solid stuff', is the basic building block of physical reality. In other words, this is a psycho-energetic universe. Far from being the misty irrelevancy that materialists would have us believe, consciousness is at the heart of the emerging new science. It is not a mere ghost in the machine, but the creative source of everything.

Mystics have always said that consciousness is the ground of all being, the fountainhead from which everything flows—and some theoretical physicists (such as Amit Goswami) have concluded that quantum physics only makes sense if we assume that consciousness not only moulds but also *creates* physical reality. This fits with everything I have taught about reality creation and the power of the mind for the past twenty years. We create everything that happens in our lives—including our state of health and wellbeing.

The well-known physicist David Bohm offered a model of the universe that was starkly different from Newton's lonely clockwork universe. Bohm viewed the universe as an undivided wholeness, like a hologram, which is forever in flowing motion—a remarkably similar vision to that of Hinduism, Buddhism or Shamanism. In his view, everything in the universe was interconnected. He wrote about the 'implicate order'—the unseen dimensions of reality—and how this unfolds into the physical universe.

God is probably another term for the implicate order—the unseen realms from which everything unfolds—though the term God has so many negative connotations that I prefer terms such as Source, Source energy, All That Is or the Universe. (I cannot push away those childhood images of a bearded, judgmental father figure in the sky!) Other popular terms for the Source are the Zero Point Energy Field (or just the Field), and the Divine Matrix. Mystics have also called it the Akashic Records, or Divine Intelligence. Regardless of what you choose to call it, the point is that the 'solid stuff' of physical reality emerges from these invisible realms of energy-consciousness.

This idea turns the materialist paradigm on its head—yet it is found in most ancient philosophies. It has been popularized in the idea that 'we create our own reality', awareness of which is now spreading to millions of people through best-selling books about the law of attraction, and popular DVDs such as *The Secret* and *What The Bleep Do We Know*. Taking full responsibility for what we experience—knowing that our lives are created from the inside out, that we are not victims but creators of what happens to us—is an inevitable consequence of living in a conscious universe. And it has profound implications for healthcare.

The new paradigm provides a scientific model for such phenomena as distant and surrogate healing, as well as 'spontaneous remission'. Newtonian physics only allows for objects to affect each other via known physical forces, and within the limitations of space and time—like billiard balls that hit each other. The new physics allows for information to travel beyond the speed of light, and to be directed by consciousness.

The new science also shows, at a deeper level of reality, that all energy and consciousness is interconnected. Wheee—such fun! This means we can heal ourselves and heal each other, as well as making our dreams come true, by aligning our energy-consciousness with that probable reality. We can also tap into any information from anywhere, beyond space and time. This opens up whole new frontiers of creative potential—and it makes sense of 'miraculous healing'.

Particles and Waves
Physicist Amit Goswami suggests that quantum physics is rather like poetry, which is why materialists have such a hard time understanding it. It is full of paradox, uncertainty and ambiguity. It swirls around in a ghost-like way, and cannot be pinned down. It also brings something as messy and nebulous as

consciousness into physics, and dissolves the old distinction between subject and object. In the new physics, we cannot be impartial observers of reality; we are always active participants.

According to the new physics, reality can behave like a solid particle *or* like an energetic wave—depending on how you observe it, and what your intentions are. This seems to be mirrored in our state of consciousness. We can have particle-like (ego) consciousness which is fixed, constrictive, limited and isolated, or we can shift into wave-like consciousness (higher self) which is more free-flowing, expansive and connected to others. *These two states of consciousness are central to conscious medicine.*

Consciousness can be like a wave or like a particle. I feel like a separate individual with my own sense of identity, yet like many people I've also had mystical experiences in which all boundaries dissolved and 'I' became part of the Oneness. At these times, my wave self seemed to *encompass* my particle self, rather like a Russian doll that holds many smaller selves within it. My consciousness expanded beyond my ego, while also holding an awareness of it, and I felt a loving sense of connectedness to All That Is. I've also had countless intuitive experiences in which I suddenly 'know' something, which my rational mind could not have known—in which I have felt connected to Source or Divine Intelligence which knows everything.

This flowing wave-like consciousness supports our health, happiness and wellbeing—as well as our creativity and intuition. Some scientists have dubbed it our 'quantum self'. The more condensed solid-particle state—also known as our ego—is linked with stress. It shrinks our awareness, and recent research has shown that it can even physically shrink our brain if it becomes chronic. It also damages our physiology and biochemistry throughout the body. We are designed to be in a wave-like state most of the time. Being in a particle state for too long is a serious risk to our mental and physical health.

Living from the Heart

One way of grasping the disparity between the old and new paradigms—or particle versus wave states—is to consider the two hemispheres of the brain. The left hemisphere is the more logical, sequential, verbal, analytical half of the brain, which sees distinctions and makes comparisons. It sees itself as objective, and is traditionally linked with masculine energy. It tends to look for differences and separateness, and prefers either/or thinking. It might be compared with the ego-self—and is the half of the brain that is identified with old paradigm thinking. The right hemisphere is more intuitive, relational, subjective and holistic. Its knowing is direct and immediate rather than verbal. It sees the bigger picture, and tends to perceive wholes and connectedness. It is more inclined towards inclusiveness, or 'both-and' thinking. It is also more tuned into emotions, sensuality and bodily awareness.

The right brain is linked with our authentic self, higher self or quantum self. It has a deep connection to our spirituality, and understands quantum physics intuitively, even if it could not verbalize it. Western society tends to overuse the left brain at the expense of the right hemisphere, and much of our emotional and physical dis-ease—as well as our leanings towards materialism—might be traced back to this imbalance.

Jill Bolte-Taylor is a neuroscientist who, at the age of 37, had the amazing experience of observing herself having a stroke after a blood vessel burst in her left hemisphere. Over four hours, she watched her brain deteriorate in its ability to process information, until she could not speak, walk, read or write, and could recall next to nothing of her previous life or identity—and it took her many years to fully recover. What is perhaps most fascinating, in her riveting account of the stroke, is that the loss of her left hemisphere gave her some unexpected advantages. All of the emotional baggage from her past simply dropped away, as did the constant drive to be 'doing', to accomplish tasks. Instead, she found herself in a state of right hemisphere bliss.

> I morphed from feeling small and isolated to feeling enormous and expansive...All I could perceive was right here right now, and it was beautiful.

Instead of seeing herself a solid, Jill experienced herself as a fluid for a long time. 'My soul was as big as the universe and frolicked with glee in a boundless sea,' she writes in *My Stroke of Insight*. Her experience has remarkable parallels with mystical experience, and does suggest that—as experienced meditators know—if only we could shut down the constant, superficial ego-chatter of the left brain, we can gain access to blissful and expansive states of awareness. As she healed from the stroke, Jill was more emotionally centered than her old self had been. She noticed how emotions felt in her body, and learnt how to hold on to feelings of joy and peace by directing her thoughts away from judgment and obsessive analysis, and towards loving-kindness and acceptance.

The left brain is our normal conscious mind (or ego-self), while the right brain has access to a far wider spectrum of consciousness. The left brain is designed for focusing, and when it is in balance with the right brain, it focuses helpfully on the positive, and on our goals and desires. But when it is out of balance, the left brain can stress and torture itself with anxiety, blame, guilt, negativity, worry, self-doubt, judgment, pretence, defensiveness and hurry-sickness—whereas our right hemisphere seems to be a doorway to states of inner peace, love, joy, compassion and authenticity. While the left brain is head-centered, our right brain is heart-centered. When the chattering mind becomes silent, we can listen to the heart.

At the Institute of HeartMath in Colorado, research has shown that negative emotions such as anxiety, blame, guilt and insecurity throw our heart rhythms into a state of jagged incoherence and disorder. When you shift your focus to your heart, and then activate heart-based feelings such as love, caring and appreciation, this induces a state of 'heart coherence', which has innumerable health benefits, affecting almost every organ and system in the body. It reduces the level of stress hormones, makes us more resistant to infection and disease, lowers blood pressure, boosts anti-ageing hormones—and has been linked with improvement or recovery from a host of physical and emotional disorders, from arrhythmia and autoimmune disorders, to fatigue and insomnia. It also helps us see things differently, so that stress-free solutions can be found to problems. In short, being heart-centered is good for our mental and physical health.

When we love and care for others—without *over-caring*, a negative state which is signaled by worry, anxiety and insecurity, along with a burdensome sense of responsibility—it also boosts our immune system. Over-caring, by contrast, is linked with lowered immune response, unbalanced hormones and poor decision-making. Caring for others at our own expense—which is characteristic of codependency—is *not* good for our health. The heart radiates love towards the self as well as others. (The golden rule is to love our neighbors *as* ourselves, not *instead* of ourselves.) When we are heart-centered, our love and care for others is balanced by self-love and self-nurturing.

In traditional Chinese medicine, the heart is seen as the connecting point between body, mind and spirit. A whole bundle of scientific research has shown that the heart has its own intelligence, which has come to be known as emotional intelligence. When we are in a state of heart coherence—when the so-called 'heart-brain' is functioning well—this seems to coordinate all the systems in our physical body and energy field, so that our physical health is supported along with our happiness and spiritual growth.

A core process that has emerged from the Institute of HeartMath is shifting into heart coherence, which I have taught for years on my workshops. It seems simple, but emerged from many years of research into how to shift out of stressful states, and reconnect with our true self. It shifts you towards the blissful, right brain state that Jill Bolte-Taylor experienced after her stroke, *without* having to be seriously ill, speechless and semi-paralyzed!

Whenever you find yourself reacting badly to a situation, or your thoughts are turning in endless circles, coming into heart coherence will help you to shift into an expanded state of awareness, and move back into your heart's intelligence. You shift into the wave response. From there, you might see the situation differently, or have fresh insights about it, or come up with new solutions — and you will simply *feel better* about it. And learning how to *feel better*, whatever the circumstances, is a key to remaining healthy or healing from any disease.

Quick Coherence

This is a rapid method of coming into heart coherence — or shifting into the wave response — which I learnt from the Institute of HeartMath. You can practice this three or four times a day, or as you wake and before you sleep, before making a decision, or whenever you are facing any challenge. If you practice this regularly, it becomes easier to remain coherent in situations that would normally trigger you into stress. It gradually entrains you to living from your higher self. If you are a health practitioner, you can use it before seeing clients or patients. The heart radiates an electromagnetic field, which affects everyone around us, so feeling good helps those around you to feel good. This only takes a minute or two, and will quickly bring you into balance:

1) **Heart focus** – *Shift your attention to the area of your heart. It might help to place your hand on your heart and/or close your eyes.*

2) **Heart breathing** – *Imagine that you are breathing in and out through your heart area. Breathe a little more deeply than usual, but let it be easy. Find your natural rhythm, allowing your breath to become smooth, calm and balanced.*

3) **Heart feeling** – *Carry on breathing through your heart while you bring up a positive heart-centred emotion—such as a time when you felt love and appreciation for a loved one, pet or nature, or doing something that you love. Or focus on something positive that happened today. Or just feel love, caring or appreciation in your heart area.*

The new paradigm of conscious medicine suggests that illness and disease are not due to a faulty or inadequate body—but due to faulty beliefs, trauma and chronic stress. In other words, disease arises from *consciousness*, rather than from the body itself. And there is plenty of evidence to support this.

Let's take the fascinating example of multiple personality— now known as dissociative identity disorder, or DID—in which two or more separate personalities (or 'alters') coexist in the same body, taking over as the conscious self at different times. Crucially, many physiological differences have been found between 'alters' in the same person. One personality *within the same body* might need insulin shots for diabetes, while another personality is not diabetic at all. Some alters may be short-sighted or color-blind, while others are not. One personality might be severely allergic to citrus fruits, cats or cigarette smoke, while other selves do not react at all. The dissociative personal-ities in a woman might have differing menstrual cycles. Alters have been found to have different brainwave patterns. One alter might be epileptic, or suffer from migraines, while others do not. One practitioner saw a woman who turned up for treatment for diabetes, which mysteriously disappeared; then she came for treatment of hepatitis, which likewise vanished. Other diseases then came and went in the same woman, all backed up by CT scans and test reports, which was baffling until he twigged that she was a multiple personality. This suggests that disease is not held in the body, but in the personality—that is, within the *consciousness*.

Claire Sylvia is a dancer who had a heart-lung transplant in her mid-forties. After the operation, she had a strange sensation that there was another presence within her. She began to crave foods that were unusual for her, such as chicken nuggets, and was drawn towards cooler colors in clothes instead of her usual vibrant oranges and reds. She began to walk differently—more like a man—was more aggressive and impulsive, and had new desires that she could not explain. Five months after the operation, she had a vivid dream about a young man called Tim, and intuitively knew that this was her donor. The hospital had a policy of confidentiality about donors, and would give her no information—but her dream slowly led her to find the family that had lost their eighteen-year-old son, Tim, in a motorbike accident. He loved chicken nuggets, and showed all the qualities and desires that Claire had expressed since the transplant.

Many other transplant patients have reported similar experiences (which gradually fade as the transplanted organs adjust to their new owner). A materialist viewpoint suggests the heart and lungs are merely a pump and breathing apparatus. The new paradigm recognizes that cells are imbued with consciousness, and that a transplant—or even a blood transfusion—is bound to transfer some of the energy-consciousness of its former owner.

If we do indeed live in a conscious universe, then healthcare that focuses on the physical body is missing the point. It is remedial medicine at best. It is ignoring the CEO of the body— which is consciousness—and instead devoting its attention to workers on the factory floor. Conventional medicine uses a reductionist model of reality that is appropriate for building a house or repairing a clock, but is inadequate and misleading for understanding people and health. We cannot keep peering down microscopes at cells to unravel the mysteries of health and disease. We have to pan back. Instead of meddling with cellular biology, we need to understand the psycho-energetic nature of the universe.

The Particle and Wave Responses

The new science tells us that there are two ways of looking at reality—both of which are valid in their own way. There is surface reality, in which everything *appears* to be solid and material, and you *appear* to be separate from me, just as a chair seems to be separate from a candle. At this level, reality is made up of separate particles. What is 'real' is limited to the world that we can see, hear, smell, taste and touch with our five senses. Then there is deep reality, or the implicate order, or the Divine Matrix, in which everything is interconnected. The deeper substrate of this reality is energy-consciousness, or the invisible realms.

Surface reality is particle-like—objects seem to be separate, and reality appears to be fixed and solid. It seems to be, well, *real*. Deep reality, on the other hand, is more wave-like—everything is more fluid and connected, more subjective than objective, and there is probability rather than certainty. And when we limit our awareness to surface reality, we get stressed and anxious.

According to the new biology, every cell in your body has two modes that it can switch between—and these two modes correspond to these two states of consciousness.

The first mode is a state of relaxed, happy and easy alertness in which healing and growth take place naturally. This is known as the relaxation response, the healing response, the love response, growth mode or 'being in the flow'. It is how you felt on that tropical beach when nothing else was bothering you, and every cell in your body switched into the relaxation response. I call this *the wave response*.

The second state is designed to keep you alive during those rare times when you are in physical danger. This mode has been called the fear response, being 'out of the flow', in protection mode or (most commonly) the stress response. It is what I call *the particle response.*

When you are looking through the eyes of the old paradigm—through the eyes of the ego, or conscious mind— you see yourself as a particle. You are focused on surface reality, and see yourself as separate from other people and the world, and even from your own body. You forget that you are a child of the Universe, no less than the trees and the stars. You feel small, insignificant, lonely and disconnected. You are often worried and anxious, never knowing what might happen next, and wanting to stay in control. Time seems to press in on you; there is never enough time—or it drags on when you want it to pass. You focus on tasks and lists, rarely living in the moment. You are easily threatened or blame others for how you feel, and might focus on what they are 'doing wrong', or what bad things might happen. In other words, thinking like a particle throws you into the stress response.

When you see through the eyes of the new paradigm— through the eyes of your heart or soul—you shift into the bigger perspective of quantum reality. You feel more like a wave than a particle. Time feels more flowing and expansive. You feel connected to everything. It isn't that you lose your sense of self, but rather that you expand around it. Being a wave *encompasses* being a particle—just as a wave is part of the sea, yet is still a wave with its own position in space-time. You are fearless in the wave response. There are no enemies, only friends. You feel relaxed, loving, appreciative, joyful and creative. Life seems effortless. There are no problems, only solutions. There is no fault or blame. Even the concept of 'healing' makes no sense from here; you are already healed and whole, and you know it. You are also deeply intuitive, knowing things far beyond the limitations of your five senses.

When your consciousness is fully coherent in the wave response, free from any fear or inner conflict, it feels wonderful. Boundaries and limitations dissolve. You become One with something greater than yourself. This is the state of an artist who is creating a masterpiece in oils, a sculptor who has become one with the clay, a top athlete who is breaking records, a scientist lost in exciting research, an inspirational public speaker through whom words are flowing, a mother cuddling her newborn baby, a toddler splashing happily in the mud, or two lovers who merge in ecstasy as they make love. You are in the flow.

Being in the particle response or the wave response is not an all-or-nothing state. It is a continuum. You might be eighty per cent particle and twenty per cent wave in this moment, or forty per cent particle and sixty per cent wave. However, most people have a characteristic range—and emotional and physical health will be mirrored in how separate you habitually feel from your heart and soul, or how connected you are. The closer you are to being a wave, the more loving, relaxed and joyful you will be. The closer you are to particle-like consciousness, on the other hand, the more fearful, guilt-ridden, mistrustful, disappointed, frustrated, angry or despairing you will feel.

Why is this relevant to conscious medicine? *Because your emotional and physical health rests not upon your genetic inheritance, but on whether you are habitually in the stress response or the relaxation response.* If you maintain a wave-like state of consciousness, you will have radiant health and vitality. The more you slip into particle awareness, the more vulnerable you become to dis-ease.

Health and the Particle Response

Whenever you feel under threat—of any kind—an avalanche of changes occur in your body. The amygdala in your mid-brain fires off danger signals, triggering the body into a cascade of neurochemical events, which are designed to deal with an emergency. The HPA axis—the hypothalamus, pituitary and adrenal glands—is instantly primed to prepare your body for action.

Adrenaline, cortisol and other stress hormones now flood into your system, preparing you for a fight or flight response, making you feel hyper-alert. Your heart rate and blood pressure increase. Blood drains away from the visceral organs and towards your arms and legs, so that you are ready to run. Your digestive system shuts down. There is no point in digesting a meal if you're about to be eaten! Your immune system switches off. While that tiger is looking for a meal, there is no point in fighting off a virus, or even healing a wound! Growth and maintenance processes in your body come to a near-standstill. This is a biological survival mode—which is perfect when you are facing a hungry tiger, since nothing else matters in that moment. Your life might depend on it.

The particle response also affects how your brain functions. Blood drains away from the frontal lobes—your higher thinking—and moves to the more primitive parts of the brain. The conscious brain cannot react quickly in a crisis. It is designed to focus, and can only process a maximum of twenty bits of information at a time. The subconscious mind, by contrast, can process up to twenty *million* bits of information per second. So in an emergency, the subconscious mind takes over. We go on autopilot, and launch into habitual reactions based upon the fight or flight response. (This is why time appears to slow down or stop if you are about to have a car accident. Everything goes into slow motion, and you seem to have endless time to react to what is happening. Your subconscious, which lives beyond the limitations of space-time, has taken over.) This means that when you are under stress, you are in a trance-like state. You become less conscious and therefore less human, more like an automaton—sleepwalking through life.

Wild animals are rarely in the stress response for long. A

lioness strolls towards a herd of grazing impala, and the herd goes into amber-alert. Is the lion looking for a meal? If she crouches in readiness or begins to run, the herd's stress response goes into red-alert, and they take flight. They bound away at full speed until they are a safe distance from the predator, then return to grazing. All of their physiology reverts to normal, and the crisis is over. Wild animals live in the present moment, and once a threat has passed, they quickly return to a relaxed state.

People are different from wild animals. We have those pesky things called *thoughts*—and it is our thoughts, rather than external stressors, which create chronic stress. The particle response was designed for those rare emergencies in which we can take immediate action to protect ourselves from a threat: a hungry tiger; a runaway vehicle; a madman with an axe; thin ice collapsing beneath our feet; real physical dangers in the here and now.

However, most of our stress comes from situations in which fight or flight is not possible, or is inappropriate—and in which you are not in any real danger. You just *feel* as if you are under threat, because of stressful thoughts: a computer crashes; your child becomes sick; a deadline looms; you face a long super-market queue or a traffic jam; an elderly parent goes into hospital; dozens of emails scream to be answered; the roof starts leaking; you get a batch of final demands on the same day; the car is making strange noises; your partner comes home late from work, and seems distant and distracted; the boss makes a critical comment or talks about downsizing the company, and you wonder whether your job is safe; you feel threatened, overwhelmed, burdened, helpless or disempowered—and your stress response is turned on.

The threat is not physical. It is psychological. You feel at risk of being disapproved of, or criticized, or abandoned, or emotionally hurt, or not being able to meet others' demands, or you feel frustrated because you are 'wasting precious time'. You feel worried about loved ones, or concerned that money will run out, or anxious about losing control of a situation. Or you tell yourself you have too much to do in too little time, and if you don't get it all done.... What? It is unlikely that the world would stop spinning, yet from the particle response you cannot think clearly. You rarely face your fears head-on, and ask whether they are realistic. You feel like a hamster on a treadmill. You are running on autopilot—too fast and too hard, and not very smart.

The threat does not even have to be a current psychological threat. We human beings are so clever that we can stress ourselves out over what happened last month, or even twenty years ago—and over events that haven't happened yet, and might never happen! ('But what if...?!') One reason why so many spiritual disciplines urge you to 'live in the moment' is that stress is rarely in the here-and-now. It is mostly in our heads.

Negative thoughts can go round in our heads obsessively, releasing stress chemicals into the body which are not needed for fighting or running away, and which only do us harm. Unfortunately, people can grow used to being in chronic stress—our neurochemistry habituates to it—so that it feels 'normal' to feel tense, anxious, guilt-ridden, resentful or overwhelmed. *And when the stress response is chronically activated, you are heading towards disease.*

Disease Begins with Dis-ease

Within the paradigm of conscious medicine, disease always begins with dis-ease, which means it begins with stress and negative thinking. Over the past thirty years, research in psychoneuroimmunology has firmly established links between stress and almost every major disease—including heart disease, strokes, diabetes, allergies, hypertension, gastrointestinal disorders such as peptic ulcers and irritable bowel syndrome, autoimmune disorders, arthritis, cancer, infertility, sexual dysfunction, muscle tension and pain, and a weakened immune system.

Crucially, the body cannot heal itself while you are in a stress response; nor will it fight off bacteria and viruses effectively. There is no point in repairing a wound, fighting off a flu virus, or even scavenging for cancer cells when you are facing a hungry tiger! The immune system uses up a lot of energy—so whenever you have stressful thoughts as if you are facing an emergency, your body puts your immune system on the back burner. This not only makes you vulnerable to chronic disease, but also means that healing slows down or even becomes impossible.

Bruce Lipton and other 'new biologists' have shown that our *consciousness* controls our biology, turning the stress response on or off, moment by moment. We are not controlled by our genes, but by our perception of our environment. Our DNA is merely a worker on the factory floor, which manufactures proteins as required. The cellular membrane is a middle manager, paying attention to signals from the environment. (Do we feel safe, or under threat?) What is more, the signals from thoughts are found to override biochemical signals from the body. *The CEO of the body is our consciousness.* We are not helpless victims of our genetic inheritance. Genes cannot turn themselves on or off. We do this ourselves. What makes our genes faulty is chronic stress—which is created by our thoughts and beliefs.

In *Molecules of Emotion*, biologist Candace Pert suggests that the body *is* our subconscious mind. The body mirrors all that we are holding at a subconscious level; and since body and mind are inseparable, it makes more sense to talk about the body-mind. A dynamic network of communication within the body-mind—known as the psychosomatic network—unites the nervous system with the endocrine, immune, respiratory, digestive and other systems. Her pioneering research showed that this network is linked up by information-carrying substances—peptides, hormones and neurotransmitters—which she calls the 'molecules of emotion'. Much of the information never reaches our conscious mind, but we *feel* it through our emotions.

Whenever we feel the negative emotions associated with stress—such as frustration, guilt, loneliness or despair—our body-mind is being pumped full of bio-chemicals which are damaging to our health. When we feel positive emotions such as unconditional love, joy, passion, hope and appreciation, our body-mind soaks in healthy biochemistry. This is why falling in love has often led to miraculous healing—and why long-term meditators tend to live longer and healthier lives. Feeling good switches off the particle response, and allows your body-mind to heal—or to remain healthy!

Healing and the Body-Mind

Albert Einstein said that, 'The field is the sole governing agency of the particle'. In other words, the invisible world (mind, energy, spirit) is what shapes and controls the visible world of matter. This invisible world—which was thrown out by science in the seventeenth century—is now being reclaimed by the new physics and new biology, and it lies at the heart of conscious medicine. The old paradigm suggests that the body is a biochemical machine controlled by genes. The new paradigm says that *the body is an energetic reality shaped by the field of consciousness.* It is our perception and beliefs that control our biology.

For this reason, when I had a diagnosis of breast cancer three years ago, I did not pursue the conventional route of surgery, chemotherapy or radiation. I looked at where my consciousness had become stuck, and what needed to shift in my energy system. For me, shifting the tumor made little sense, since this was not dealing the roots of the problem—and might even mean that I would miss a vital opportunity for growth and change. I committed myself to a journey which would honor my body's needs, and which felt joyful and self-nurturing—and to address the very obvious issues that had created the cancer. And the cancer healed.

For me, the field of healthcare and medicine is becoming a potent force in helping us shift towards a bigger picture of reality—and I believe we are now creating so many diseases which conventional medicine can do little about *in order to help us shift* to a higher state of awareness. In the twentieth century, seeing a disease as psychosomatic was tantamount to saying that it was imaginary, that it was 'all in your mind'. We are now realizing that, apart from a tiny proportion of disease that is present from birth, every illness is psychosomatic. In a psycho-energetic universe, what matters most is what we think and feel. This is the world of conscious medicine.

Within a conscious universe, the human body—rather than being controlled by genes and biochemistry—is dancing to the tune of consciousness and subtle energy. This is then *mirrored* in changes in our biochemistry, neurology, organs, muscles and physical structure, even in how genes are expressed. In other words, what happens at a physical level is merely a symptom of what is occurring at higher levels of organization—just as we can begin to affect our physical health in moments by connecting with our higher self. Within this new model, changes in the body 'unfold' into physical reality from the invisible realms of energy-consciousness—this is exactly what cutting-edge research in biology is demonstrating. And as awareness of this spreads, we are seeing more and more 'miracles' in which people with so-called incurable disease become fit and healthy again—simply by shifting their energy, and changing their *minds*.

The relatively new field of energy psychology offers thousands of anecdotal reports of healing. The most widely used form of energy psychology is EFT (Emotional Freedom Technique). This was popularized as the 'five-minute cure for phobias'—which made me skeptical at first. It was only when I saw a women being cured of chronic asthma in less than a minute that I knew I must train in this strange-looking technique! That was in 2001, and since then I've used EFT in many hundreds of sessions with clients. Although healing can take hours or even weeks rather than minutes, EFT almost always has a positive impact, and can be mind-boggling in its speed and effectiveness.

Gary Craig, creator of EFT, often said that EFT was 'the ground floor of the new healing high-rise'—and already there are developments from EFT, which take energy psychology into a new dimension. Countless other healing techniques, which are based upon shifting our energy-consciousness, are also being introduced, such as Matrix Energetics, Theta Healing, The Lifeline Technique, Reconnective Healing, Quantum Shiatsu, Zero Balancing, The Yuen Method, BodyTalk, ZPoint, Quantum Touch, Nutri-Energetics System (NES), Holoenergetic Healing and the Body Code. All of these lie within the field of conscious medicine—and such approaches promise to transform healthcare forever.

A New Beginning

Many have called this the Age of Awakening, or the Age of Consciousness, and ancient prophecies have pointed to this era as a time of transformation. Some visionaries have even suggested that we are becoming a new species: homo spiritus. For me, 2012 is not an end-point. Instead, it marks an exciting new beginning—a time when enough people on the planet have 'woken up' spiritually to make a real difference. Quite often, this awakening comes in response to a serious diagnosis or other life crisis.

Many different disciplines and theories are now converging to bring us a stunning new view of reality, which has huge implications for healthcare and medicine. We are stepping into a conscious universe. As we come to inhabit this new world—as we shift towards a higher level of consciousness, and release the limiting beliefs, struggle, fear and victimhood of the past—healing from *any* disease becomes not only possible, but more and more probable. Instead of being seen as a problem, illness or disease becomes a meaningful message—and even a precious gift. It can be a stepping-stone towards conscious evolution.

Note: Gill Edwards contributed this chapter from her new book, *Conscious Medicine* (Piatkus, 2010).

Chapter Nine

The Maya Prophecies for 2012

Miguel Angel Vergara

Why did the Maya leave written Prophecies in their books like the Popol Vuh, Annals of Caqchiqueles, Chilam-Balam, and Mayan Legends and Traditions?

The Prophecies or predictions were written in their Sacred Books by the Maya as a warning, a call to conscientiousness, to generate a level of knowledge, and above all a consciousness and understanding of the different events that are occurring at this time on our planet.

The state we now find our planet in is very delicate. The imbalance and disharmony caused by irresponsible actions and the unconsciousness of humankind in general, has required that Mother Earth herself begin a process of 'Auto-purification' in a natural form in the planet.

The Maya called our planet *Kaban*, which translates from Maya to English as the *being* of the earth. This concept tells us that the Maya knew that Our Earth was a living being who feels and was the keeper of our life. All of our actions result in her wellbeing or her destruction.

In these times, we are getting close to the end of a great cycle of 26,000 years, in which our Sun has traveled through the twelve Constellations of the Zodiac. This Cosmic movement relates to the return cycle of the Sun of Alcione, located in the Constellation of Pleiades, known by the Maya as *Tzab-kan*, translated to mean, 'Constellation of the Serpent's Rattle'.

The Maya called themselves 'The People of the Serpent'. The allegory or symbolism of the serpent with the wisdom and sacred knowledge is very obvious. The Maya Masters also knew that the Pleiades Constellation influences, in an important way, the physical, emotional, mental, and spiritual behavior of humankind through the energetic influence on our Planet Earth.

In the last years, our Sun has generated intense Solar Rays, causing high levels of radiation and great agitation in all living beings on the physical, emotional, mental, and spiritual levels. The reception of these high levels of light and energy is making the energetic frequencies in our Planet, and all that lives on it, adjust to them. Many of us are now asking ourselves:

Who are we?
Why are we here?
What is our purpose in life?
What is our true mission according to our present experience on Earth?

The Earth is changing, not as a punishment, but as a great opportunity to rectify our conduct, our attitudes towards life; doing this leads us to recuperate our consciousness, our love, respect, and our truth towards all living beings in the marvelous planet on which we live.

The Maya Prophet, Chilam-Balam, tells us:

We are not alone here on Earth.
There are great spirits who live in the animals, plants, trees, in the water, in the stones, and everything that is created. If we allow them to die, we will follow.

The Ancient Maya indicate that in this moment there are ancient beings, Masters of Light, Spirits of Light, who are amongst us to help us care for and honor the Spirits in the same way that Nature cares for them, without affecting or damaging them.

If all of us unite with love and respect in a circle, in

community, and accept and practice the wisdom of our Maya ancestors, we can acquire the wisdom necessary to confront the events that are occurring on the planet today with wisdom and harmony and—acting with consciousness in our daily life—we can channel positive energies, cosmic and telluric, natural and human.

Remember that:

We are creators able to think, to create, and to manifest.

Mother Earth supports us, nourishes and protects us, as long as we do the same for her.

We all have a cosmic responsibility for the planet and for the entire creation.

We have the capacity to change our life, our destiny! Today!

We still have time; it is not too late. We can do it with faith and positive determination! Now!

The Maya legends, passed down from their oral traditions, have allowed us to discover their root messages that offer us the opportunity to better understand the Maya's theories of the evolution of the universe and therefore to more deeply decipher their Prophecies.

Everything has a beginning and one of the first questions people ask is about the origin of the Maya: Where did the Maya come from? The oral traditions tell us:

They did not come from anywhere on the Earth or the Sea. He whose name is whispered in a breath brought them here...

Here, we face the Cosmo genesis of the Maya; the gods created the Maya people right here, on the lands of the Mayab. The Maya didn't come from anywhere else, but were created on this land:

> He whose name is whispered in a breath, namely, God/Goddess, Father/Mother, who symbolizes the Divine Breath. So just by breathing, each time we inhale and exhale, we are pronouncing his Sacred Name.

Regarding the cycle that we are now living in and its end in December 2012, the Maya prophet Chilam Balam tells us the following:

> Every moon,
> Every year,
> Every day,
> Every wind, walks and passes also,
> Everything returns to the place of stillness...

Everything in the Universe is cyclical, which is why the Maya say:

> Everything passes and walks.

In the words of Don Alejandro Cirilo, from the ancient tradition of the Maya Quiché:

> We were the Maya,
> We are the Maya,
> We will be the Maya...

Past, present, and future are one; time and space do not exist as such.

Now, the cycles can be extended if the consciousness of

human beings awakens—and then, together, we can consciously unite with the Spirits of the Guardians of Nature and with the Elementals. If we take care of them and love them there is no doubt that the cycles of time will be extended for our Mother Nature and we will be provided with more opportunities to be in harmony and balance with her... We must remember that what is outside is inside... And what is inside is outside...

We have all earned this right, to work in love and respect for the harmony of Mother Earth: every day, each moment—and with every thought, every word, every action.

That is why the Maya said in their prayers:

Holy Earth,
Holy Water,
Holy Air,
Holy Fire,
Holy Spirit...

Since everything is holy, each grain of sand, each stone, tree, animal, human being, cloud, river, sea, mountain, and volcano—well, everything—is sacred, because everything in life is provided by the great Creator of the Universe, the Father/Mother. Everything arises from that source of light, from the Creation, from infinite love, harmony, and respect.

Let us return to that sacred energy. Now is the moment...

Who were the Maya? The sacred books of the Maya answer:

They were holy men, filled with wisdom and each one of them was known to the gods...

They were beautiful, brave, and gave love and mercy...

They built the temples tall and gleaming so that the men

from near and far would come to worship He Who Has No
Name and is above...

They raised the great white buildings so that the Masters
could teach the Wisdom...

Many times, we have asked ourselves how was it that the Maya
could build their pyramids, temples, and monuments in all the
Maya area, an area now understood to be approximately 350,000
square kilometers. And according to actual statistics, the number
of archaeological sites, or Maya ceremonial centers, surpasses
20,000, and each site contains between ten and 1,500 pyramids or
temples. To imagine the architecture of this great culture is truly
a marvel, a great feat. It is mentioned in their legends that they
were teachers of the Wisdom, of the Sacred Knowledge, which is
what made this degree of evolution possible in this culture.

One of the great Teachers was Itzamna 'el Rocío del Cielo',
the Dew of the Sky. Here is his story:

Señor Zamna, the Father of All, was among them, his hand
performing the Wonders of the World, standing high above
them to direct and lead them. And he cured them of the ills of
the body, and gave them the light of the sun to ignite their
spirits so that they would always be connected with the sky.

They say that Zamna was one of the most holy and wise priests
from Atlantis and that on a special date he received from the lips
of the High Priest of Atlantis, the following message:

The Gods have communicated to me that on the next full
moon our earth will sink...Go and choose the good and the
wise and bring them with you to a new land, where under
your guidance they will once again prosper...

They came from Atlantis to the Land of the Mayab, today Yucatán. Mayab, means in the Maya language, 'The land of the few', 'The land of the Chosen Ones'.

So, in this era, before the sinking of Atlantis, Zamná chose a few and arrived in the land of Yucatán, which they named Mayab. When Zamná arrived to the Land of the Mayab, he built the beautiful cities of Izamal, Chichen Itzá, Uxmal, Mayapán, and Dzibilchaltun, among others.

He named each village, each ceremonial center, and taught the people about astronomy, mathematics, calendars, the recording of the stars in the sky, and how to work with the Earth and its elements; how to love and respect Nature and all the living beings in it.

The legends about Atlantis tell us that it was when they built temples to honor the human body of men and women that the third eye stopped functioning...

Internal fires have destroyed the Land of our Fathers (Lemuria) and the Water threatened the fourth Race (Atlantis)... The first great waters came and submerged seven islands... the good were chosen and saved...

It is good to know that in these times there are voices from the ancient tradition of the Maya that speak to us of what occurred and of what can occur to Humankind.

One of the prophecies, told by Don Alejandro Cirilo Oxlaj, seventh generation priest of the Quiche Maya, says:

'The human race must find the Path of Initiation in the Earth and in the Sky. The Spring Equinox of 1995 marked the beginning.

During the night we can observe the pyramid-house of Hunab-Ku and, in Spirit, visit Tepau, Gukumatz, and HuraKan, our creators who can direct us to the House of God.

Together all of them pray, meditate, and work with the Sacred Light of the brightest star in the Orion Constellation, called Belatrix, in order for its light to illuminate the people of Earth... Through this initiation they will be able to lead us to see the luminosity of the Great Spirit.

When this Initiation is completed in the House of Hunab-Ku in the sky, the Spirit of each initiate will be illuminated and return to Earth.

Chichen Itzá, Izamal, Uxmal, Tikal, Palenque, Edzná; all these Maya Sacred Centers, have a specific function to awaken the seven powers.

Only through the Initiation of the Human Body will it awaken...

This is why in this moment the Maya Teachers of Light implore all the Sacred Human Hearts to awaken, for it is the only way you can fulfill your Sacred Destiny: to be true sons and daughters of the Cosmic Light.

When the Time of Knowledge approaches, the light in the center of the pyramid-house of Hunab-Ku ignites and pierces the shadow that envelops the human race...'

Another Maya Elder, Don Pascual of the Maya Quiché Tradition, who follows the great tradition of the Mayan Calendars, tells us the following:

We Ah-Men (Shamans), as guardians of the tradition, have a special commitment, which it to keep track of time, to count the cycles, since in each one of these is written the history of the world. And in each turn or bend in the infinite spiral of the Great Serpent Kan, there is always a return, which gives us similar events, so from this it is possible to know our destiny. For as we know the paths of the Sun and Grandmother Moon, which come and go every day, as we humans come and go, we know how to cast lots and anticipate events...

In the year 1987, I was with my Maya Teacher, Don Vicente Martín Guemez, in the upper temple of the Pyramid of KuKuulKaan at Chichen Itzá, when he said to me:

> Miguel Angel, I see millions of people coming to visit Chichen Itzá—each one of them, whether consciously or unconsciously, coming to receive a Seed of Knowledge, a Seed of Consciousness, which he then carries in his spirit back to his place of origin... Chichen Itzá, will become the Maya Sacred Site, where people share Love, Wisdom, and the Light of the World, with all humankind.

Today, Chichen Itzá has an average of 3,000 people visiting daily.

Today, his vision, his words, are a reality... Awaken! Now is the time! Act now!

Chapter Ten

The Teachings of the Serpent and Mayan Prophecy

Teressena and Martien Bakens

More than any other creature, the serpent is most consistently found in ancient cultures around the world. From ancient Sumerian and Minoan artifacts, to Indian, Egyptian and Mayan texts, you will find the symbol of the serpent. The spiral shape of the coiled serpent is perhaps the most widespread image carved on ancient Celtic dolmen, among Native American petro-glyphs and etched on pottery vessels in Africa and Australia.

Why is the serpent such a universal symbol? What did the serpent mean to all these ancient civilizations? Why was it so prominent? And what does it have to do with the Mayan prophecies we are hearing so much about?

While much has been written on the serpent as the symbol for the Goddess and the divine feminine, and while there are many references to the serpent as the kundalini energy in both sexuality and spirituality, there is little reference to the serpent and the cosmos.

For several years we have had the honor of working with Don Miguel Angel Vergara, a renowned Mayan elder and nagual. He tells us the ancient Maya were the keepers of the cosmic knowledge and wisdom. They called themselves 'the people of the serpent'. This description refers to their star-ancestral connection with the constellation of the Pleiades (Tzab-Kan), which is seen in the heavens as the rattle at the end of the tail of the serpent. The serpent itself is the Milky Way. The energy of this cosmic serpent brings the transmission of knowledge and wisdom from the cosmos to the Mayan people.

The Olmec people, of the Veracruz and Tabasco area of Mexico, predate the Maya. According to our friend and teacher Jesus Fabian Ortiz, Olmec refers to 'the people who are the rope that connects to the stars' or 'the movement of the rope in the universe'. Here again, we find reference to the serpentine energy of the cosmos.

John Major Jenkins, in his book, *Mayan Cosmogenesis: 2012*, refers to the serpent rope as a wormhole or star gate. He states that the writings of Egypt, Sumeria and Tibet also refer to an opening in the center of the galaxy; out of the center the serpent rope emerges, and riding upon it is an enlightened being.

Compare this idea to the image of the serpent-entwined egg commonly used in ancient mystery schools. The egg represents the embryonic state of physical existence and the serpent, the mysteries. At the time of initiation, the shell is broken and we emerge as the newly realized soul.

The ancient mystery schools understood this connection of the serpent and the cosmos. Manley P. Hall, in *The Secret Teachings of All Ages*, writes:

The coils of the snake have been used by the pagans to symbolize the motion and also the orbits of the celestial bodies, and it is probable that the symbol of the serpent twisted around the egg ... represented both the apparent motion of the sun around the earth, and the bands of astral light, or the great magical agent, which move about the planet incessantly.

The ancient Maya were incredible astronomers with profound understandings of the workings of the celestial bodies. Mayan day-keepers passed down this knowledge through the ages. Today, we are in the midst of a rare thirty-six year journey of the earth. For the first time in 26,000 years, the earth will be closest to the galactic center and the sun will be most closely aligned with what is known as the Dark Rift, or the Black Road of the Milky Way. For the Maya, while the Pleiades represent the tail of the serpent, the Dark Rift represents the mouth of the serpent. Through sacred ceremony, Mayan shamans would enter the serpent's mouth, traveling through the darkness, until they reached the eternal source of the infinite. In this place of cosmic consciousness they were reborn, coming back through the passage, bringing cosmic knowledge and wisdom to the people. This was not merely by the sharing of their experience or the words of their stories, but as living conduits of the energy received, bringing these celestial frequencies with them to the earth. When you see the images of the feathered serpent, Ku-Kul-Kaan, you will see the face of a man emerging from the mouth of the serpent. This is the truly true man, the enlightened one.

In this amazing time in which we live, we are about to pass through this Dark Rift. It is an opportunity for all of us to enter into the ocean of cosmic consciousness of the Great Serpent. Within this space, we experience unlimited possibilities, expanding into our full potential as multi-dimensional beings. We are one with Great Mother, one with Infinite Source. The manifest and un-manifest, time and no time, are interchangeable and equally present. Our ability to shift between spirit and matter occurs through the attunement of our hearts to the heart of the Earth and the heart of the Sky.

In his teachings, Don Miguel shared with us an aspect of the Mayan prophesies as given to him by five of the Mayan elders of the Inner Council in Guatemala, connecting with the Mayan Teachers of the Sky. At this time that the prophecy has indicated, they expect the return of Balam-Eb. *Balam* means the messenger of the stars, teacher from the Pleiades. *Eb* means link with sky and earth. It is believed they were on earth originally and gave humankind the knowledge. Now is the time they will return and we must have the proper frequency to receive them—the frequency of love.

They tell us that at the time indicated in the prophecy, Venus will fall down in the West, the Pleiades will rise in the East, and Orion will be in the North. As our solar system crosses through this Dark Rift, we may experience three days of darkness. When this happens, it will signal the end of this age and the rise of a new age, the Age of Light. Alcione is the sun in the Pleiades constellation and the vibration of Alcione is ninety-nine per cent light. This is one reason why it is so important that we come face to face with our shadow side. As within, so without. We also must pass through the darkness in order to receive and reflect the light of this next age.

A personal experience to share here occurred at the sacred site of Palenque, deep in the jungle of the Chiapas. *Nah-Chan-Kaan*, as it is known by its Mayan name, means 'the house of the Serpent of the Infinite'. We were facilitating a group journey with our friend and teacher, Don Miguel. Miguel had shared with the group that this is the place 'where Wisdom's children are born.' It is the place 'where you will be born into the serpent's cosmic wisdom'.

On this day, after our initial ceremony at the Temple of Inscriptions, we visited the Temple of the Mother, one of the smaller structures with an exquisitely carved panel depicting a woman birthing. She is the representation of the feminine principle of creation, Ix-Cheel, Mother of Childbirth, Divine Mother. From there we proceeded to the Temple of the Foliated Cross. While we are standing there, an incredible blue light appears at our third eyes. It is as though this light generates an energy field around us that creates a multi-dimensional portal into timelessness.

There is an otherworldly quality that compels us onward to the Temple of the Cross. As we ascend the temple stairs, stopping at each of the nine levels, there is an air of high ceremony, and remembrance of having walked these steps before in past lifetimes. With every step, there is a deepening, a strengthening of our union as twin flames. And though there is an awareness of every step as a step of initiation, there is an ethereal sense of floating outside our body, outside time and space.

At the top of the temple in the sacred chamber, we begin to tone. A tremendous energy pulses through us, a swirling flow of cosmic energy coming from the infinite expanse of the universe. Again, an incredible blue light surrounds us, creating a powerful shift in consciousness. The initiation is complete.

We descend the Temple of the Cross, still in an altered state. Don Miguel and the rest of the group are waiting for us. It is near closing time of the site and we begin the trek back to the entrance. Don Miguel, who is leading the way, turns around and smiles: 'The Temple of the Cross is the place of initiation of the Truly-true Man and the Truly-true Woman,' he announces.

It is difficult with words to describe what we experienced at Nah-Chan-Kaan. Perhaps its name says it best of all: 'the house of the Serpent in the Infinite.'

This aspect of the Infinite is central to the Mayan prophecy of 2012. Our perception of time and space, as we experience it in the third dimension, will expand into greater possibilities of timelessness. At this moment in time, it is like we are in the space between the worlds, between the cosmic in-breath and out-breath.

Patricia Diane Cota-Robles, founder of New Age Study of Humanity's Purpose, Inc., offers a beautiful explanation of this event in her article entitled, *What Now?* She writes:

Once every several billion years, celestial and galactic cycles within cycles dovetail into one rhythmic pulsation. For an awesome moment, this unique pulsation brings all life into cadence with the heartbeat of the cosmic I AM—All That Is.

During that cosmic moment, our omniscient, omnipotent, omnipresent Father Mother God inbreathes the whole of creation into a higher octave of evolution. This Cosmic Inbreath is known as the Shift of Ages.

The Maya calendars are the key to these cycles. They do not record linear time, but rather the rhythms and vibrations of the energies that each day brings. Part of the prophecy talks about returning to the 13/20, reminding us to attune to the energies at play in the cosmos.

Why does the number thirteen carry such a negative connotation in the Western World? Why is there not a thirteenth floor in most buildings? Why is Friday the thirteenth considered unlucky? Anytime something is vilified, we need to truly ask ourselves why this is so.

Thirteen is associated with the divine feminine through the lunar aspect of thirteen moons. The thirteen Moon calendar assists us in attuning to the natural patterns and cycles of the earth and heavens.

In the celestial signs of the zodiac, how many people are familiar with the thirteenth sign or Ophiuchus, the Serpent Holder? Ophiuchus, originally called Serpentarius, is one of the original constellations identified by Ptolemy, appearing in *Al Magest* Star Catalogue (c. 130 – 170 A.D.). Ophiuchus is a sun-sign in the Real Solar Zodiac. The sun can be seen against the stars of Ophiuchus between November 30th and December 17th each year. As such, it falls in the position between Scorpius and Sagittarius.

On either side of Ophiuchus lie the two parts of the serpent he holds, *Serpens Caput*, the Serpent's Head, and *Serpens Cauda*, the Serpent's Tail. The myth associated with Ophiuchus tells us he learned the secret of the Elixir of Life from the Serpent. The story of Ophiuchus, the Serpent Holder, embodies the serpentine energy as the sacred energy of the eternal. Like the

Serpent Holder, we hold the key to our true divine nature. Our serpentine energy is called the kundalini, which lies at the base of the spine. Through the activation of the kundalini energy it is possible to ignite our divine blueprint as beings of pure love and pure light.

The image of the Minoan Snake Goddess depicts the goddess holding a serpent in each hand, reminiscent of the image of Ophiuchus. This Minoan sculpture represents the Great Goddess, the Earth Mother. The serpent is the creature closest to the Earth Mother, feeling her heartbeat as it is belly to belly with Gaia.

This wonderful piece dates the civilization during the Bronze Age, around 2700 – 1450 B.C. The fact that these ancient civilizations knew of or had a depiction very similar to the image of Ophiuchus shows us a number of plausibilities. One, they knew of the importance as related in this story to what can be seen as part of creation—the Mother holding the creative propensity, to bear new life. Another is that the Minoans remembered or never forgot the oral history that connects them to the Celestine events now catapulting our society in our own remembering. Then we may yet consider the stories that connect her with other rites. Minoans mainly had female figures as Goddesses, which may be why they depicted Serpentarius as a female. Today, these images are re-emerging in our consciousness as we remember who we truly are.

While there is much discussion around the prophecy of 2012, it is actually the time beyond that is really of interest. What happens in 2013 is up to us. What we choose to collectively co-create as the vision of the fifth world. We are all here at this time to dream the dream alive. It is time to let go of the old paradigm that limits our perception, not only of time and space but also of possibilities, and embrace the cosmic consciousness of our becoming. It is time to enter with the whole of the Earth into the Dark Rift and emerge as the truly true beings we are and always have been.

Life is a continuum, represented by the serpent that eats its own tail, the Ouroboros, reminding us of the continual cycles of death and rebirth that occur time and again. We are passing through one such cycle where the Earth and all her inhabitants are poised for rebirth, recreating a new sense of who we are and our place in the cosmos.

H.P. Blavatsky writes in *Isis Unveiled*,

Before our globe had become egg-shaped or round it was a long trail of cosmic dust or fire-mist, moving and writhing like a serpent. This, say the explanations, was the Spirit of God moving on the chaos until its breath had incubated cosmic matter and made it assume the annular shape of a serpent with its tail in its mouth.

The same chaos is moving and writhing again. We have been in an incubator, about to emerge and embark on a grand journey beyond 2013. In our collective human journey, certain people are the way-showers; they simply pick up on the energies which universal consciousness sends out before others do. They set the stage, so to speak, for the greater part of consciousness, the rest of humanity, to catch the drift or, in this case, the rift. The hundredth monkey is simply a larger group following the creative principle inherent at this time.

As talked about by Xel Lungold, when it is such that the collective consciousness is following what the Maya have called 'the evolutionary steps of the pyramid of our soul', it becomes apparent that we are on course with our creative destiny. This pyramid model outlines the levels of consciousness we have experienced in our collective human consciousness. Each level or step of the pyramid spans a period of time indicating a cycle of days in which each 'day' is metaphorical, representing the time frame in which our evolving consciousness takes place.

During the time span of the last level, leading up to December 2012, the ninth step of this pyramid, the days separating the nights, indicate a time span of only twenty days long. In the previous level, the one we are currently in, the day length is 360 days. Within each level, the 'days' become exponentially shorter, which is why we feel time speeding up—we are in the quickening, about to birth a new era. As the days get shorter at each level, it creates the form of the pyramid, becoming narrower at the top. (For more information: http://mayanmajix.com/lab_F1.html)

At the present time, we are in the Galactic level of Ethics, where things previously hidden from the light are now revealed. The collective consciousness of humankind desires truth and right relationship with all that is.

The coming level is the level of Collective Co-creation. Within this level of consciousness, we have the ability to envision our new reality together and dream the dream alive. Already we are seeing the alignment of the many grassroots organizations all over the world, slowly but surely weaving their threads together. While these organizations started out small, they have grown over the years into substantial entities, and collectively we are changing the way we do business, the way we interact and the way we live our lives. It is indeed a wondrous time in which we live.

Our most recent work, *The Fifth Tarot*, is an evolutionary new tarot deck created in unity consciousness that works with the energies we are experiencing as we move through this Shift of the Ages. As the manuscript and artwork evolved through divine guidance, we felt our participation in the collective vision that is being called forth at this time. In the past year, we have traveled to twenty-nine states and four countries presenting the teachings that came through *The Fifth Tarot*. Everywhere we go we find the afore mentioned parts of the equation in action, people coming together to synergistically change the way we live and relate to each other and the world around us. Through our travels, we have encountered a great number of way-showers who have answered the call put forth by universal consciousness, and are putting into motion and followed through with what was asked to be done. In a greater 'knowing', they have collaborated with their awakening blueprints and have engaged the main hard drive, moving us safely closer to what lies beyond the next level of the pyramid, beyond 2012.

There was much gratitude and joy in our hearts when we were asked to collaborate on this book. It is this same gratitude we experience each morning upon waking to hear the birds sing and enjoying every moment of that day. It is the same joy we feel every time we do a tarot reading, offer a shamanic healing session, or do the work we were called to do in the form of writing, creating, or drawing.

The awakening is moving us closer and closer into oneness, to the divine principle the masters have spoken about. We are living at a time when we are all asked to be the greatest we can be, to boldly go where no 'man' has gone before. Funny, how science fiction becomes part of our reality. Equally amusing is it when the reality we create lies far beyond what any one person might perceive as science fiction.

As we near the end of the fourth world and are about to enter the fifth world, we are proffered an enormous opportunity. Through the gateway that opens before us we can create anything — and will. When we come through this transitional time we will look back and say, 'Wow! What a ride!'

In the course of that statement, many of us will be in different experiences, enjoying the expressions of Divine as it presents itself to us, as we dream them into being with our strong intent or with a group's intention. When the journey leads us to a place of unity consciousness, we may never have to experience the aspect of duality or struggle again, as we remember our divine nature and return to the veritable Garden of Eden. Let's all enjoy the journey and continue to build with the unfolding energies and see the castles of our hearts' creations.

Chapter Eleven

So? Live 2013 Now!

Dr. Jim Young

Back in January, 2006, two friends and I initiated the Arkansas Metaphysical Society (ARMS) in Eureka Springs, AR. We sensed, surely, that there must be more than the three of us who would enjoy discussing matters related to the expression of inner Truth rather than duality-based ego consciousness. This turned out to be true, and years after initiating meetings for this purpose our group of faithful participants still meet for two hours every Monday evening. As facilitator for the group, when we get off to matters that relate not one iota to spiritual consciousness—the ordering of Life from the still, small voice found only inward—I am prompted to ask this one, simple question: 'So?' When sinking to the level of debating opinions and beliefs, I raise this question only to assert that we have strayed from our central purpose: to live each moment only in the now—by seeking Wisdom inwardly and living true only to the spiritual order Wisdom imparts to our lives when faithfully followed.

As I have to come to understand some of the issues and concerns dealing with the end of the Mayan calendar, it has become clear to me that a similar prompt could prove helpful in framing the new level of consciousness beginning to influence us in the here and now. Without doubt, we need not wait until 2012 for a new level of consciousness to arrive. Neither do we need to wait for 2012 to begin living it.

Just as it is when facilitating ARMS, my purpose is to shift the perspective on the issues and concerns related to the date of

December 21, 2012 just enough to inspire some deep meaning to be heard within each of us, hopefully so we can more fully discern how such information is to influence our lives. Truth lurks just beneath the surface, waiting only to be made aware. Sensing on some level of existence that the source of Wisdom awaits our presence, we come thus to understand our only imperative is to listen while deeper meaning seeks our awareness. And then only to surrender to each single roar of Truth on the path we are to walk, to demonstrate as our legacy to the world.

Let's now see how this approach plays out with the information and views we have read thus far. We'll begin with a more surface view and move deeper and deeper, until we can see our way beyond simple outer appearance.

To summarize, we are told that it is likely that there will be a confluence of many external factors impacting our lives in and around 2012. For example, we are told that the Mayan calendar contains a date—December 21, 2012—a date and time portending the end of life as we know it. I would certainly hope so. This prophecy is akin to the Biblical expression that tells us: 'We cannot see the face of God and live'. What comes from within me as I hear this Biblical declaration is quite another sensibility: 'We cannot see the face of God and live *as we have lived*'. Likewise, our perspectives about life are shifting so swiftly and so dramatically these days that we cannot continue to live as we have. I hold the same to be true as we go within to discern the deeper meaning of all the outer signs related to 2012, the signs that relate to the fulfillment of some prophecies; prophecies, I suspect, that are as unfamiliar to the Maya as inner Truth, Wisdom, is to many of us.

Also, we are told that in 2012 there will be an increase in sunspot activity, strongly influencing the energetic configuration of our planet. Then there's the suggestion of breaches in the earth's magnetic field, which could lead to a reversal of the magnetic poles. Other projections speak of 2012 as a time when our planet will align directly with the sun and the center of our galaxy, an event supposedly taking place only once every 25,800 years. There is likelihood, it is said, that the earth will spin wildly off its 23 1/2 degree tilt of center and roll over, causing worldwide volcanic eruptions and massive changes in the structure of our oceans, destroying all life as we know it. This could be scary stuff, except scientists tell us, for example, that this alignment already took place in 1998. Other physical elements are also cyclical in nature and have ebbed and flowed through the centuries, and they still do. We could not stop any of them then, and we certainly cannot now.

When tying the ending of the Mayan Calendar to the destruction of our planet in 2012, I am tempted to ask only, 'So?' If we look at the endless prophecies that have predicted the end of our planet at a given time and in certain ways, we readily see that not a single one has come true. Here we are, still. Could it be that this record of prophetic failure on the physical plane speaks to the end of life on another dimension—the end of utilizing the more superficial levels of consciousness from which we often draw life?

As another example of 'evidence', the hieroglyphs from Maya antiquity tell stories. So? Are these stories about the Maya culture or ours, and for what purpose? Certainly, their glyphs, like those found in Egypt, in the Southwest and elsewhere, *do* tell stories—about the natural evolution of a society's spiritual consciousness, as is true for *all* cultures. In this case, the stories the glyphs depict are not even uniform among various locations in the Maya culture, so how could any single one of them be right for us? Don't you think it's rather narcissistic to make these stories all about us?

Then, of course, there are those who benefit by our collective and individual compulsion to engage such information and live from fear rather than going within to our center of peace and equanimity. The end-timers and those who espouse Armageddon as the sure and final chapter for us all would hasten this so-called impending disaster, so they could ascend sooner rather than later, leaving the rest of us behind. And let us not forget those who gain financially by producing and selling goods and services to those in a state of vulnerability and fear, repeating a practice seen at other times in our history.

Again I ask, 'So?' So, none of these views, elements or potential influences are any of our business, not at all. How others want to envision and live their lives is up to them and we need to respect that right. However, respecting their right to differ doesn't mean we should take on their ways and beliefs as our own. Our single imperative is to listen inward and follow only the direction found inward. By doing so, we not only bring spiritual order to our lives, we inspire others to follow our example—so we can join in walking in our Truth rather than in what others want for and from us.

To be sure, there *are* influences on our planetary life, but worry cannot change any of them. To be sure, worry never fixed or changed anything. No matter how many potential influences others speak of creating a threat to our well-being in 2012, the only practical thing we can do is shift our perspective about them, and to understand if we live only in this moment, true to our inner guidance, this is the very best we can do for ourselves—and all around us. It strikes me that the Serenity Prayer used in Alcoholics Anonymous fits perfectly here: 'God, grant me the serenity to accept the things I cannot change, the courage to change the things I can and the wisdom to know the difference.'

We cannot change these disruptions that may affect our planet, but we can change how we see the planet, and behave accordingly. When we take a broader view, we come to see it is fortunate that such potential forces in our lives do have an impact on us—do inspire us to consider if we are doing all we can to live compassionately and holistically.

As an example of seeing life from a spiritual perspective—symbolically—if we were to take the prophecies as metaphors, the only natural disasters they really speak about are our commonly held inner catastrophic thoughts, obsessions and addictions—all speaking to the level of fear and sense of separation we carry within us. Much like sunspots or storms, abiding various aspects of fear speaks to the emotional storms that darken our natural state of light, and which are highly disruptive of a peace-filled existence. These elements also constitute the highly limiting beliefs and opinions of others we have come to depend on for our validation, identity and direction. Prophecies of good or enlightenment reflect going inward and following the One True Voice, Source, God, Truth, Christ consciousness—whatever name one wants to put on the small, still voice heard only inward. The name matters not, for when we strip away the name or label we find only our common divinity holding us in highest regard, and which has only highest good in store for us.

Surely, our world *is* turned upside down when we are moved to such deep levels of being—and well it might be. Moving from the superficial elements of ego consciousness and self-importance to the essence of our very Being can be earth shattering, to say the least. Yet, on this deeper level, Wisdom enlightens us as we comprehend with spiritual clarity that prophecy is about one's holy relationship with our inward Truth, Wisdom—called God by some—and nothing else. On a spiritual level, prophecy is not about some physical happening or likeness. Transcending to spiritual or Christ consciousness frees us from spiritualizing ego consciousness—from making outer appearances look spiritual, when they're only akin to a wolf in sheep's clothing—and takes us to ordering our lives from a spiritual foundation found only by listening inward.

Over the ages, this is the inward journey that mystics and

visionaries have encouraged us to take. Surrendering to deeper awareness is what allows for transcendence of Spirit over matter, and frees the demonstration of a new perspective. With the new perspective comes deeper meaning and a sense of spiritual purpose, as never before witnessed. The Truth of our spiritual essence is reinforced yet again. To paraphrase what *A Course in Miracles* suggests, a life of feeling separate from God or our own divinity began when we *forgot to laugh* the moment we first heard the suggestion that we are separate.

As Einstein told us, we cannot solve issues and concerns on the level at which we find them. We must look in another direction—discern the causes on another level. From a spiritual point of view, all we need do in this regard is to discern inwardly—to remember we are spiritual, divine beings, and can focus anew on seeing life from the spiritual perspective.

This life is not about depending on what we have been told in our past, or fearing we won't have what we desire or need in the future—for one is history and the other, mystery. Neither is now. Neither the past nor the imagined future is pertinent. When aware, we know without reserve that all there is to live is each successive present moment of now. Yet, in large numbers, we continue to think living the collective consciousness about such matters is still the way to go. It is time to *change* the collective consciousness. The time has arrived to dump current beliefs and opinions about all these potential 'problems' and instead demonstrate the abundance of Truth we have available to us.

The changing state of consciousness is either more, or less, helpful at any given moment, just as the development of our own spiritual consciousness unveils itself over time. Both cataclysmic and inspirational moments and periods result as we rid ourselves of the old beliefs and opinions, and as Truth takes up the slack. Upheaval is necessary if we are to transcend our current way of life. This upheaval too shall pass—and peace of mind and divine order will prevail once again.

When all is said and done, we come to the ultimate conclusion related to scientific predictions or prophecy: when we apply The Inward Journey scientifically—without fail—we find we have not only a failsafe means for living in what may appear to be tumultuous times, but we also will have discovered the purest means of living lovingly. And, just as with any other scientific evidence, we can observe the results with accuracy and regularity.

As we develop our inherent capacity to deal with life from a spiritual foundation, outer appearance or authority will have no influence whatsoever on our lives. Whenever such outer declarations are made, we don't ignore them. We simply take them for what they are—and then go inward for spiritual direction, so we can live safely in spite of the apparent outer influence. So, you see, no matter what 2012 holds for us, we would have the spiritual foundation in place for dealing with it responsibly—for the highest good of all concerned. Who could ask for anything more?

So? So, what's the path we are to follow? Well, are you living by the will of others for you and out of your ego conscious self? Or have you discerned that life is lived more wholesomely from the inside out? There is only *now*, an unceasing array of present moments to live and to demonstrate our commitment to a new level of living. The beginning of a new commitment to live in the now is here, not somewhere else.

If Life has shown me anything, it has shown me there *is* a better way to live: A way Emerson called self-reliance, by following our intuitions, moment by moment, day by day; a way Shakespeare posed when he asked, 'To be or not to be? That is the question;' a way Rumi suggests to us in his poem:

Out beyond ideas of wrongdoing and rightdoing,
there is a field. I will meet you there.
When the soul lies down in that grass,

165

the world is too full to talk about
language, ideas, even the phrase *each other*
doesn't make any sense.

I call this better way, 'The Inward Journey.' It is a way the Maya point to in their teachings about spiritual consciousness—just as Jesus did, and other spiritual leaders before him and since. Let's be careful with the term journey, however. If we see the journey as some kind of seeking or as a way to achieve some reward at the end of the journey, rather than simply Being in our awareness, we will have missed the point. Seeking and material reward holds us in ego consciousness both feet planted; we only seek when we think we're separate from what we really are— and we want reward only if we fail to see life from a spiritual perspective. When we see ourselves as divine instead of separate from our divinity, we know without fail we *are* the journey; we *are* awareness demonstrated.

What I'm suggesting with this approach—now that you have some idea of what resonates within you as Truth from all the information about 2012 you've taken in—is for you to remember and demonstrate your natural capacity to live from the inside out. Once you shift your perspective in this direction, it's like erasing time between now and 2012—assuredly, into 2013 and beyond—and simply acknowledging your spiritual discernment so you can live the Truth or Wisdom beckoning you with regularity, moment by moment, throughout eternity. The result of your commitment to living in the now is that you will be living in the very same now in 2013—and beyond—for now is all there really is. Let's take a look at what this could mean for you and all around you.

Listening for and surrendering to the inner voice is what brings spiritual order to Life, and this ordering is what we are asked to consider as the foundation for metaphysical discernment. The level of spirituality I'm speaking about here refers only to the consistency with which we connect inwardly—with our own inner voice—Christ consciousness. Many of us take being spiritual to mean we must study some religion, live in an ashram, be a vegan or at least a vegetarian, meditate, do yoga, and/or have some other special practice or job. While all of these can be helpful and nourish us greatly, in and of themselves they do not constitute being spiritual in the context I'm providing here.

The height of spirituality is reached by staying aware of our connection with the Holy Spirit, spiritual or Christ consciousness—our highest self—not some outer source many have come to call God. Any god found 'out there' is a false god, a god found in separation, a mere idol we supplicate ourselves to and petition for one favor after another. There is no real difference between such a god and Santa Claus or the Easter Bunny.

In a metaphorical sense, when we look at Scripture for assistance, we come to see that Mary, the mother of Jesus, represents the clarity of discernment that says something inside us informs us of the Truth we are to demonstrate—and which brings spiritual order to our lives. Jesus symbolizes the commitment one gives to spiritual discernment with all one's mind, body, spirit and strength—and living true only to this single voice. Spiritually speaking, there is no Truth but this Truth, no way but the inward way—the inner journey—no path to follow but the straight and narrow—no path to follow but your own True path; you and your path are One. It is not the prize at the end of the journey that is important. The importance is to know that we are to *be* the journey—and to savor the journey and the journey alone. This is simplicity at its best.

To cut to the chase, the most authentic form of love we can muster begins with love of Self, meaning love of the Truth we are to follow. When we live faithful to demonstrating the Truth, Wisdom heard inward, we bring our authentic Self to others and all we do, absent of ego involvement of any kind. What could be more loving—more honest, more authentic—and more intimate? What might our lives look like if we began each day comprehending the fullness of our divinity and living only from such a clear understanding of ourselves? If we add the power our example would give others—so they, too, might live true to themselves—a legacy of major proportions would lay stone upon stone on the foundation of spiritual reality.

We arrive thus at the spiritual definition of compassion. Many think compassion means we should fix others, or at least fix their condition or circumstances, no matter what they desire in the matter, no matter what they know their purpose to be. We substitute our beliefs and opinions for their welfare, as though we have change as our charge—and as if we had the wherewithal to do so in the first place. Fixing others or their conditions is more about pity and arrogance than compassion. And it's more about vanity, thinking we're separate from God and one another, rather than fully comprehending that *all* of us are the perfect image and likeness of divinity and therefore don't need fixing. All we need do is help one another to *remember*—to *remember* with our inherent divine nature and to act only from this sacred space. And to hold all in that remembrance the same.

Expressing compassion for ourselves means we follow inner guidance rather than outer authority—or our own beliefs and opinions—for our life's direction. Thus is humility defined: giving up self-importance—'I know what's best for me and others'—for the Truth of any matter or circumstance, discerned as the infinite gifts of grace imbedded in simple awareness on our part. Compassion for others means that we respect the dignity of all, including plant and animal life, also seeing them as divine. Out of our divinity, we honor divinity common to all. In Sansrit: Namasté. 'As divine, I also celebrate and honor your divinity'. In Maya: In Lak'ech Ala K'in. 'I am another you, God'. These greetings simply and sweetly convey our acknowledgement of real love and respect.

How do we develop our innate capacity for listening while deeper meaning awaits our awareness? All any of us can do is tell what works for us, but you must discern for yourself how you hear the voice of intuition or inspiration and become enlightened. The best I can do is to explain to you what I've done to become more open over time, and hope it ignites your own inner catalyst. I hasten to say this to you: the still, small voice I speak of is the voice of inner peace and joy. It appears as a sudden, deep knowing, like when intuition strikes. An 'aha moment', when insight and enlightenment arrive. When you go inward to find Truth or Wisdom awaiting you, if you hear instead of Truth your 'inner critic', or get a feeling of fear, angst, doubt or worry, these are *not* the inner voice I'm talking about. Those feelings and source of guidance represent only the voices of ego consciousness, those clamors of distraction we still need to transcend, so spiritual Truth has room to be heard and move through us.

A friend says it this way: 'How do you know it is Truth you hear? It is Truth if the knowing of it sets you free.'

But it is not Truth itself that sets us free. If this were so, Truth is all there is, so why don't we all feel free? Fact is, it is *the knowing* or *our awareness* of Truth that sets us free. This is why it's so important to practice connecting with and following Truth. (For an in-depth description of the process I have used to develop 'The Inward Journey' approach for myself, see my books, *As If From God* and *Aware in a World Asleep: A Principled Way for Living Spiritually*. www.creationspirit.net.)

The importance of this approach to living an extraordinary life in an ordinary reality is to more fully comprehend that by doing so we are building our capacity to live and demonstrate our lives in the now. Moment by moment, we listen to our inner voice for life's direction, thus surrendering our age-old dependence on the distractions of outer influence or the voice of opinion and belief for life's direction. This we know for sure: whatever level of consciousness we begin any action with is what will manifest in our lives—and very quickly nowadays.

The Law of Order says to us that whatever consciousness we abide with intention and focused attention will demonstrate that precise result in like kind. So, if we remain in ego consciousness and focus our lives on outcomes driven by competition, need for power and collections of material goods beyond our actual need, then our day to day world will look exactly like that: full of power games, competition, failed relationships, collections of goods we don't need and, generally, a life of chaos.

Should we decide that abiding ego consciousness is obviously not what inspires us to be what our heart calls us to demonstrate, we can begin each day with the sure inner knowing that we are divine. Divine: the Universe of spiritual or Christ consciousness, the frequency or vibration of love. When we begin our commitment to Life out of divinity, we then demonstrate each loving inspiration coming to us as insight, intuition and enlightenment. No matter what we call what informs us, follow it we do, demonstrating one loving act after another, and our hearts fill with joy and our minds come to peace. Indeed, we have all we need within us to fulfill ourselves as beings of the loving way.

It seems to me that the main thing is to keep the main thing the main thing. Precisely what is the main thing, you ask? The main thing is to remember we are divine—to re-member *with* divinity—and when we order our lives by going inward for direction, we live the fullness of spiritual reality, of Truth, our divine purpose and calling. Duality then falls away from our lives. This may seem like a complex 'main thing', but in reality it is very simple. It's as simple as this: we all have an inherent calling to fulfill. We want to be in touch with the calling so we can responsibly bring it to fruition. When we lose touch with spiritual reality, Soul calls us to return to harmony—working in us as our own awareness, as well as prompts from those who genuinely see us for what we are called to deliver to the Universe.

Our natural longing to be expansive, to live, to learn, to contribute what we can, to love, and to Be are reflections of Spirit's purpose—so Spirit's image and likeness can come to Life. When we bring order to Life through spiritual presence, Life becomes a Self-fulfilling prophecy. Indeed, each inspiration, when heard and followed, is prayer being answered, demonstrated into fulfillment. Prayer is something we *hear*, not something we mouth to petition with. There are no exceptions to fulfillment when ordering comes from spiritual alignment. Congruence with the voice of Truth, the voice of Wisdom, occurs only when we silence our own beliefs and opinions. When we do silence our beliefs and opinions, all those issues and concerns we formerly gave weight to—like those tied to 2012—no longer take precedence over living spiritually.

Through the seemingly discordant times of our lives—before we break out into the light of our spiritual awareness—we are much like the fuzzy caterpillar that spins a chrysalis around itself. Spun out of the threads of our beliefs and opinions, and encased in self-importance, we form a protective shell around ourselves—which becomes the face we put out into the world, the clothes that shield our Truth from all around us, even from us. And yet, within this shell there is quite another voice calling us—calling us to be what we really are: divine. Sensing on this deeper level that living out of ego consciousness is not really living at all—while at the same time knowing we are engaging with some magnificent transcendental process—we give way to simply being with our true inner calling until we are ready to burst out of our shell and dance in our magnificence.

You see, although we occasionally rest in seeming darkness, some essential spiritual images are not only regularly nourishing us, but also are preparing us to break out of old, more familiar patterns. Now aware of those essential ingredients assimilated with little notice on our part, we free ourselves of the outer shell of beliefs and opinions, and we come to live day by day in the fullness of our enlightened being. Much like the majestic Monarch butterfly, we break out of our chrysalis and dance about in the extraordinary beauty we now feel safe giving to the world around us.

This is the inner journey we all are called to take and live by—and to Be. Liltingly, we embark on this inner journey fully aware of the deepening affects it has on our lives, as well as those around us. The inner journey lights our way, and reveals the beauty awaiting only our awareness and demonstration, just as with the Monarch butterfly which inspires us.

So? So, let's celebrate the fullness of life by gathering in common understanding that although appearing different, we are One. By helping one another to see the fullness of our inherent divine nature, we also affirm the behavior that demonstrates divinity into every day being. To paraphrase Wordsworth, 'We are lent to one another this way'. Divine order thus lights our way. The world is all the better for it—and uplifted by it. Indeed, we can fly—and fly we will. Who among us will be the hundredth monkey? Or is it really the hundredth butterfly?

By demonstrating our lives from this seat of love, we see all others as divine and treat them with the respect for the dignity they deserve, even if they don't yet see themselves as divine or treat themselves as though they are. We exercise relationships and business ventures collaboratively rather than competitively—the pinnacle of a win-win approach. We respect each person's inherent right to exercise their own inner agreement for the life they wish to live, instead of imposing our judgments and desires on them. Life demonstrates a lavishing of love on one another rarely seen in our time. And along the way, the fear that creates duality fades into the distance.

Just as importantly, we come to live more fully in the now, with little or no reference to any part of our past or what we might want in the future. Both history and mystery vanish from our lexicon. Only each moment of now commands our attention, and we hone our capacity to live just this way, no matter whether in 2010, 2012, or beyond—into 2013 and beyond even then. When living spiritually, it doesn't take long to comprehend that we aren't living in any particular time at all, and spiritual order is brought to each moment of the only time there is. Joy and peace replace a timepiece watched. Without doubt, we can live 2013 as if it *is* now, for now is *all we can live*, no matter what else is said about it. Undeniably, living in 2013 begins right here!

Chapter Twelve

A Tomorrow Unknown

Nicolya Christi

With the drawing of this Love and the voice of this Calling, we shall not cease from exploration. And the end of all our exploring will be to arrive where we started and know the place for the first time through the unknown, unremembered gate.
T.S. Eliot

Many people across the globe are sensing a powerful urge to let go of the past and yet have no idea of what to let go into. Many are realizing their jobs, their homes, the locations they live in and their current relationships no longer reflect who they are. We find ourselves in a paradox. We are not sure where to be or what we want and yet know that we are dissatisfied with our lives. Rather than focusing on what we do not know, it would be more beneficial for us to focus on *what we do know*. What we do know is that our lives no longer seem to fit the person we are becoming. Many of us are finding it impossible to plan for a future. 2013 presents to us a blank canvas on which to rewrite the story of our lives.

Since the total Solar Eclipse of 1999 many people have begun to realize that humanity is in a transitional phase. We find that as we move closer to 2012, everything that relates to our old ways of living is losing significance. Many of our cultural stories, creative art, music and the media relate to outdated modes of thought and expression. By remaining connected to these old ways, we keep ourselves locked into the past and held back from a future bursting with potential. We are being encouraged to live in the *now*, not as a theory or an ideal, but as a reality. The fact is that over millennia, humanity has been conditioned to need to *know*, but where has this led us? By living in the *unknown* we can experience liberation from agendas, expectations and conditioning. We stand on an exciting threshold of uncharted territory.

Suffering verses Freedom

We are moving from the Age of Pisces into the Age of Aquarius. The Pisces archetype has been teaching us to transcend suffering, to learn forgiveness, to develop compassion and to love unconditionally. As we continue to move from the Age of Pisces, these key areas are brought to our awareness even more. Are we still experiencing suffering? Are we able to forgive with ease and grace? To what degree have we developed compassion? The fact is that we attract into our lives the very circumstances that allow us to heal, integrate and evolve. We have a golden opportunity to take a giant leap forwards in 2012. Now is the time to let go of the past and our conditioning and turn towards the future to live a life that uplifts, liberates and empowers us.

It is vital that we learn to move on and not turn back and look over our shoulder. Humanity has become so accustomed to suffering that we do not realize the extent to which we have become conditioned to it. Astonishingly, suffering has become an accepted part of our lives because it is all we have ever known. Suffering has embedded itself deep within our personal and collective psyche and we need to acknowledge that we have an unconscious attachment to it. It is suffering that binds us to the *known*, which has become a refuge for safety; yet it is just that, a place of refuge, not our home. We are afraid to move out of our comfort zones. Our attachment to the known fosters an unhealthy need for security, albeit a false one. We each carry wounds of loss or abandonment. We each carry what psychospirituality refers to as the 'original wound' —*separation from Source*. This is the core wound that lies at the root of all suffering.

When we are disconnected from God/Source, we are disconnected from ourselves and we experience suffering. Many of us have been raised to believe that Jesus died on the cross for our sins, which further alienates us from God, as we unconsciously battle with the collective guilt of two thousand years. Wars are waged in the name of God, misinterpretations of religion distort the path to God and laws have been made that have nothing to do with God and everything to do with the manipulation and control of the masses.

At a deeply unconscious level, suffering has become an addiction and a habit. To transcend suffering we need first to acknowledge that it is there. To gain an idea of the degree of relationship to suffering, pause for a moment and feel your way into the personal and collective suffering around you. Having done so, now make a conscious, focused and *felt* statement such as, '*I acknowledge the presence of suffering within my own conditioned mindset and in the world around me.*' This allows us to take the first step towards freedom.

Our current world culture is unconsciously addicted to suffering. We are weaned on it, we are educated by it and we are raised in it. Suffering is all around us, no matter where we go or what we do. We are conditioned to believe that suffering is a natural human state. Most of what we see, hear or speak of has suffering woven into it. Modern culture does not realise to what extent it is still immersed in suffering. Once we acknowledge the degree to which suffering permeates *every level of existence* here on the planet, we can consciously choose to remove ourselves from this perpetuating cycle.

Are we not bored with what is on the menu of life? Does the old adage, '*familiarity breeds contempt*', not apply to our lives? Why do modern lives revolve around alcohol, drugs, sex and money, which mostly serve our escapist tendencies? What are we escaping from? Are these our attempts to avoid suffering? The paradox is that the tactics we use to avoid suffering only result in entrenching ourselves further in an unconscious reality. We limit ourselves to a third-dimensional world, where our altars are our televisions and our main connection to spirit comes through a bottle.

A good place to begin to address our addiction to suffering is to let our imagination take us back in time to when suffering might have first begun. We do not need to have a cognitive or intellectual understanding of the history or nature of suffering; we can simply pause and feel, pause and feel, pause and feel as far back in time as our *felt* memory permits. For a moment, allow yourself to travel back hundreds and thousands of years. Allow yourself to observe momentary flashes of wars and persecutions, the pillaging of the Earth's precious resources, dictatorships, slavery, genocide and the endless ancestral stories of suffering. Let your imagination observe scene after scene and acknowledge what you are aware of.

All of what you register (and so much more) is tantamount to the amount of suffering that has been held unconsciously within your psyche, for we carry forward what has gone before, not just in our personal ancestrally linked memory, but also in our link to the collective memory. Simply by acknowledging just how much suffering has befallen humanity you can begin to release it from your personal memory and disconnect from the collective memory.

Psycho-synthesis (a humanistic and transpersonal psychotherapy) promotes the need to *identify* in order to *dis-identify*. However, we need to find a way of revisiting the past in a way that does not re-traumatise us, and so induce more suffering, as so often is the case when we share a painful memory. It is vital to our healing to locate a trauma origin imprint, yet if we can do so without re-traumatizing ourselves, we can effectively begin to heal ourselves of an unconscious addiction to suffering. I encourage us to share our stories of trauma in no more than seven to eleven words. By using more than seven to eleven words, we can find ourselves becoming re-traumatized, which also affects our bio-chemistry. So we can say, for example; 'I was abandoned as a child', or 'I was abused when I was ten'. Leave out the detail and instead focus on how we feel in the *here and now,* what feelings are alive within us now. Going into the detail puts us in our heads. Focusing on the feelings allows us to acknowledge, be with and heal them. *In order to heal, first we must feel.* We do not need to re-traumatize ourselves to heal; in fact, by doing so, we take ourselves further away from the healing process.

Reflecting on the origins of suffering allows us to gain some perspective about the extent in which we are still held in suffering, which in turn keeps us locked into the known. The known is 'safe', yet not fulfilling. The known is a familiar place built upon our need for security. We experience *fulfilment* when we feel at one with nature, Spirit and ourselves. In modern language, the term 'fulfilment' has developed an entirely different meaning from its true one. We mistakenly associate fulfilment with safety and security.

Fulfilment is a *feeling* of profound proportions. When we know what fulfilment *feels* like, our lives become transformed, as we move into *trust, surrender, gnosis, openness, loving kindness, forgiveness, compassion, sensitivity, creativity and unconditional love.* When fulfilled, we experience each day as a great adventure, we live in the moment and we are excited by the prospect of the unknown. Fulfilment has nothing to do with security or the known and everything to do with living in the moment and the unknown.

For modern humanity, true fulfilment is a rare experience. When did you last feel fulfilled, and by this I do not mean secure or safe? My sense is that the closest most human beings come to fulfilment is when a parent holds a much wanted newborn for the first time, an experience that may fade quite quickly as the demands of the known take hold again. You may believe that you know true fulfilment in moments of intimacy. Is that really true, and if so, how long does that feeling last? When you are sexually intimate with your partner, do you merge with the Cosmos, Spirit with Spirit, Soul with Soul, heart with heart, body with body until no separateness is perceived and there is only Oneness? Such a union is a transcendental experience and allows us to know what true fulfilment really feels like.

Fulfilment is a spiritual experience and any lesser experience may result in your being content for a short time and, at worst, left feeling empty. We can experience moments of fulfilment through self-love, and loving others, meditation, creativity, in fact, any experience that engages the heart and calls forth the soul. Security can be bought and paid for, whereas fulfilment is the blessing of a pure and unconditional heart.

We have become addicted to what those in power tell us we need. These are not authentic needs that resource and empower us, such as a need for love, to express our feelings, to be seen, heard, held, acknowledged, valued and appreciated. We also have fundamental needs for shelter, food, warmth and safety. We have adopted 'pseudo' needs that are not our own and are instead the needs of global systems, which, by numbing us to the fact that we are suffering at a personal, collective and spiritual level, maintain ultimate power and control over our lives while we remain a part of their systems.

T.S. Eliot's *'Unknown, unremembered gate'* leads into the field of dreams. To enable us to stand in that place, we are required to trust, surrender, have courage and faith and live in the moment with neither one foot in the past nor in the future. The place of the unknown is the dominion of the *Now*. It is the place where we *let go-let God* and where our personal will has aligned with our higher Will. When we arrive at the unknown gate of remembrance, we *remember* who we are and that we no longer need to suffer or to remain locked into the collective pattern of suffering. In the place of the unknown, life effortlessly provides all that we need.

Stepping into the unknown requires total surrender to the path of our hearts and the wisdom of our souls. We need to recognize that we have confused the meaning of safety with security. The first serves our survival needs, and the latter our material needs. But what of our spiritual needs?

A radical transformation of global, environmental, ecological, social, political, economical and financial structures is necessary. This becomes a possibility when we reclaim our empowered, authentic selves. If we were to relinquish our personal and collective attachment to suffering, the current dysfunctional global system, which perpetuates suffering, would collapse.

We can learn to live in a different way, one that serves life, each other, nature and the planet. How can we transcend a history of suffering if we support the very system that keeps it in place? By becoming aware and elevating our consciousness we can break the hold the system has over us. Most people exist in a waking sleep, caught in patterns and routines that keep them secure, yet deeply unfulfilled. By acknowledging this, they could change their lives.

It is time to embrace the spirit of adventure that *is* the unknown. We can usher in a New World structure built upon honesty, authenticity and integrity. Our consciousness is the coal waiting to be fashioned into a diamond. We must let go of both unconscious and conscious attachment to suffering. It can be as simple as flicking a light switch. We need only make up our minds to do so. Suffering belongs in the past. Do not allow it to keep you from your golden future. Be sure to leave suffering behind as you cross the 2012 threshold, through the unknown, unremembered gate that leads to true fulfilment.

Waking up

Many of us are finding our way to the writings of inspirational New-World thinkers and those at the cutting edge of consciousness. These include, Dr. Ervin Lazlo, Greg Braden, Geoff Stray, Alberto Villoldo, Jose Arguelles, Terence Mckenna, John Major Jenkins, Daniel Pinchbeck, Sharron Rose, Solara, Celia Fenn, Karen Bishop, Ronna Herman, David Wilcock, Drunvalo Melchizedek, as well as websites such as Worldshiftmedia.org, Positivetv.tv and many other extraordinary sources that signpost the way ahead in these momentous years leading up to and beyond 2012. Such information helps us to understand why we feel the way we do and guides us in navigating our way through these times of great change and uncertainty.

The time has come to write a new story for our lives and to let go of those handed down to us by our families and our cultures. These are not our stories; they do not belong to us. We must hand them back with love and write our own. You are being urged to become *aware* and *informed* and, by doing so, help to educate and prepare others for the transformation of human consciousness in 2012. Both the Earth and humanity are ascending to a higher level of consciousness and evolving to a higher vibration frequency. Ultimately, ascension is about the creation of Heaven on Earth.

The profound Earth changes, astronomical events, astrological aspects and the culmination of ancient prophecies—which all converge in 2012—contribute to a higher vibration quantum field (divine matrix). As a result of this raised frequency, our consciousness and physical bodies are undergoing a transmutation process. We are shifting from duality to unity consciousness. For too long we have been disconnected from the soul, living our lives from a personality level. The process of ascension will serve to realign the personality with the soul.

Collectively, we are living in a time of confusion and anxiety and this is also being experienced at a personal level by many of us. Most of the changes we are experiencing as a result of a consciousness shift are difficult to view as positive or life enhancing when we feel compelled to end relationships, relocate, leave our jobs or totally transform our lives. Add to this the physical symptoms and experiences caused by an ascending consciousness and the impact of changing Earth frequencies and the whole process can feel overwhelming! We may feel that as much as we try to transform our lives to become more peaceful, we often experience upheaval and feel that we are moving backwards instead of making progress. This can be because our own frequency is shifting as we move from the old lower vibrating frequency to align with a higher one, and by responding to this process at an unconscious or conscious level, we invite a period of turbulence as we readjust and realign.

Many of us are feeling tired, lethargic, 'depressed', confused and frustrated. Often we find that our attempts to transform our lives appear blocked at every turn. This is a result of a realignment process to the higher frequencies that now permeate our energetic as well as our physical bodies. In order to move through the tiredness and apathy and motivate ourselves, we must flow with these new higher vibration energies. By choosing to become informed and aware, we can reawaken our passion for life and experience fulfillment. Enormous courage is required to alter our perceptions and embrace the resulting changes in our lives; however, by doing so the rewards are immeasurable. Most of us have spent years merely existing, surviving, just getting by day to day, living uninspired lives in which our true selves are barely present. Imagine feeling *alive*, being *in love with life* and knowing who you are and what you are here for? This is how we are all meant to live.

Most people will avoid change because it usually requires a sacrifice or the need to let go. Change invites us to step out of our comfort zones, which may entail entering into a period of turmoil and upheaval; it may confront us with our deeper fears and a give a sense of going backwards, not forwards. To use an analogy; the archer draws back the arrow to its furthest point of tension and then simply *lets go*. By pulling the arrow back to its maximum point of tension before being released, it is able to fly the greatest possible distance. The more we experience upheaval and the bigger the step backwards appears to be, the further ahead we will land once we are ready to let go completely and fly.

Believe in yourself. Trust you are being held and guided by the love of those in the heavens who walk with you. Have faith in your unique individuality. Embody a fundamental truth, which is that *you* have something important to offer. Adopt an *attitude of gratitude* for yourself. Trust and surrender are the keys that open the treasure chest of your soul. Believe in *gnosis*: that intuitive felt sense in which *you know without knowing how you know*. Memory, intellect and academia do not inform gnosis. Gnosis is pure knowing informed only by the heart and soul and is the highest form of human intelligence. Gnosis engages our intuition, our sense of *feeling* and reveals our true wisdom. Information is power—gnosis is *empowerment*. Too much left brain activity with its emphasis on intellectual and academic information is not conducive for accessing the sixth sense of *gnosis*. Forget what you think, and believe what you *feel*.

We are moving from an entrenchment in lower consciousness, into the embodiment of an elevated consciousness. We are moving beyond the universal law of attraction, based on cause and effect and an acquisition mentality, into the Law of Elevation, founded on higher universal laws that we are now ready to embody. The Law of Elevation will lead to the Law of Unity and Unity Consciousness—whatever affects one, affects all; ultimately, we all are one energy.

You are being urged by your higher Self to *let go and let God* and to release all conditioning, let go of the belief in struggle, in suffering and of your attachment to false security. Start to believe in the magnificence of who you truly are and what your life can offer to those around you and the world you live in.

This chapter appears essentially as it is in Nicolya Christi's new book, *2012: A Clarion Call – Your Soul's Purpose in Conscious Evolution*, available March 2011.

Chapter Thirteen

2012 - The Great Equalizer

Aluna Joy Yaxk'in

'The sky is falling! The sky is falling,' said Chicken Little.

Do you remember reading that fairy tale? Boy, I do. Do you remember Saturday afternoons, being mesmerized by the old black and white scary movies that played when we were growing up? I had nightmares about giant spiders taking over the world for years. What were our parents thinking, letting us read and watch such things?

Oh—and do you remember those atom bomb drills in school? You know—the ones where the alarm would make you jump out of your skin, while you were being asked to slip under your desk. How dumb I felt crouched under my flimsy, school desk. I knew that if a bomb were to go off anywhere near my school, I was going to be toast. That school desk was no comfort to me. It didn't stop me from wishing that my parents would build a bomb shelter in the back yard like everyone else. Hey, I was a little kid back then—and the adults should be keeping us safe, right?

Now Hollywood is making new films to scare the livin' daylights out of us! I think it is about time that we all realize that we have inherited a bum, fear-based agenda. We have been programmed from birth to believe in the apocalypse, catastrophe, judgment day, devastation, all over mayhem, and the end of the world. If we are not buying it anymore, what are we going to do about it?

About a decade ago, we created this Y2K thing, so we could

remember something really important. The fear around Y2K had tons of folks running around like powerless victims. They were running up their credit cards to buy survival supplies. They thought the world was ending, so they would not have to pay their bills. They tricked themselves into believing that they didn't have to be responsible for their actions! The ETs were going to save them anyway, right?

Just prior to Y2K, I wrote an article called *Fear is our enemy, and Chaos is our Friend.* OK, the title is a bit cheesy, but it got published all over the world. Then came the hate mail. Some called me a dumb, New Age blonde, and I was going to be responsible for people not being prepared for this horrible event. It didn't bother me. I just sat back, because I knew what was coming. Well we know what happened don't we? Y2K came and went without the sky falling or the computers crashing. A bunch of survival companies retired in luxury after this one, but many individuals were left with huge financial and karmic debts to pay.

Where was I for Y2K? I decided to run the other direction away from Y2K. I was up in the Chiapas Highlands in Mexico having a once in a lifetime experience in a little church called San Juan Chamula. The Maya people were out in full force to celebrate the millennium. We were the only Gringos there. I have never experienced anything like this since. It was powerful. Then, at the stroke of midnight, we danced in the main square to a salsa band wearing pink satin suits. It was a priceless and surreal moment. The really ironic thing was that my fairly conscious house sitter back home in Sedona felt like he had hit the jackpot. He was on my roof at midnight ready to watch the crash of the century. Yep, he had a year's worth of food stored in my house—a house that he thought I would not return to. Boy, was he embarrassed when I came home. Oh, yeah—I had a few apologies in my inbox when I got home too. That was nice.

Now we have the looming presence of a simple, but ominous,

date on the calendar. December 21, 2012. There is huge and unnecessary commotion about who is right about this date, by the way. Many are calling this time 'The end of days,' or 'The end of time.' The Mayas call this 2012 frenzy a fabrication of the Gringos. They themselves know that the earth has always changed, and civilizations rise and fall over and over again. The planet warms up and cools down with or without humanity and technology. It is a natural cycle that has always existed on the earth. Yes, it is true; we are coming to a reboot of a huge cycle of time, but this is not to be feared. This time is to be respected and celebrated. It is time for us to grow up, let go of the catastro-phobia and become the truth of who we are—and that is the co-creators of this reality! It is time to have a little respect for the resources on Earth, not because we want to save our skins, but because it is the right thing to do!

OK, let's have a serious intellectual moment here. I am not the only one who feels this way. Joseph Robert Jochmans wrote,

The Hopi and Mayan Elders DO NOT prophesize that every-thing will come to an end. Rather, this is a time of transition from one World Age into another. The message they give concerns our making a choice of how we enter the future ahead. Our moving through with either resistance or accep-tance will determine whether the transition will happen with cataclysmic changes or gradual peace and tranquility. The same theme can be found reflected in the prophecies of many other Native American visionaries from Black Elk to Sun Bear.

I admit it—I am an idealist. But I would rather shoot for the stars, and have paradise here and now, rather than dodge earthquakes, burning hot lava flows and rising oceans. Aren't we here to live in bliss and create heaven on Earth? Isn't one of the functions of the Maya Calendar to bring about harmony in all life?

Hey, don't let me stop you. If drama and scaring yourself silly is entertaining for you, go ahead and knock yourself out. But don't think for one second that December 22nd, 23rd or the 24th isn't coming, or that you won't have to pay your bills and uphold your obligations. You are the cause of your own effect! The sad thing here is that humanity didn't learn from the Y2K scare, and 2012 is taking its place. Fear is becoming big business, and I am scrambling to get out of the way of this roller coaster ride. It doesn't sound like any fun to me. If you think people made money off of the Y2K fear tactics, then watch out, 2012 is the mother of all scary prophesies, and it has just begun! Fear is very good for the economy. Watch out for the expanding number of local, corner, survival stores and the mass exodus from the rising water. I think it might be a good time to move back to the beach. No one will be there.

Many metaphysical and intellectual teachers out there are clamoring to align themselves to be the authority on 2012. Everyone wants a piece of the action. It is the old, snake oil sellers reincarnated. Even Nostradamus is rolling over in his grave wanting a piece of this action! There are the books on 2012 and the survival workshops; there are DVDs, CDs and YouTube videos telling you that the sky is falling, and if you watch this, maybe you will feel safe; there are astrologers, numerologists, meteorologists, geologists, and a whole horde of 'experts' telling you why you should buy their stuff, go to their workshops, and how you too need to high tail it for high country. Haven't we learned by now that when we go into fear that it blocks us from hearing our own inner truth? Do you want to feel SAFE? It is simple—stay in your heart and listen to the truth within. The fact of the matter is that no one could, or can be, an authority on 2012. The closest we can get to an authority on 2012 and our possible future is the Maya Elders themselves. After all, it is their culture that the date 2012 came from—or did it?

It does not matter who is right and who is wrong. We all have a right to our unique perspective. But our differences in beliefs do not change the fact that this shift is happening no matter what, and if we like it or not. Jesus said, 'Keep your lamps lit'. In other words, keep your hearts open, and be in a state of readiness, because no one will know the day or the hour. Our attraction to the 2012 phenomena is giving our overly active minds some comfort by thinking that we know what is happening. The fact is that no one knows what the future holds for us. The future does not exist. We create our future as we go — step by step.

This, my friends, is the beauty of this incredible time! 2012 will become a great harmonizer, equalizer and unifier of humanity. Egos that are tied up in being the leading authority with find themselves so far out on the preverbal limb that they will discover themselves in a huge and very real recession — the post Maya 2012 recession, that is. They will have 'cried wolf' one too many times, and this little red riding hood doesn't buy it anymore!

I am over the fairytales and the campfire scary stories. In fact, it is time that we ALL got over it, and got on with it. It is time for us to grow up and come to terms with who we are as a human race. The fact is that we are living masters, but somehow along the way, we got caught up with running away from the Boogieman. It is time for us to come back together as a team, of equals and soul family, with a common goal that supports peace and harmony on Earth. It is time to quit following the few self-elected leaders like lost sheep, and begin to follow our hearts. We have grown past the need for gurus. We are becoming living masters, so we better start acting like it. Don't you feel it is time? We have a great opportunity *right now*, and you don't want to miss it. We can come together, and begin to create a new and better world — together. We can do this without self-right-eousness, spiritual arrogance, competition or making one another right or wrong. We can also create Heaven on Earth without playing follow the leader or even trashing the leader. Maybe this time we can get down to the real reason why we are ALL here—and that is to create paradise together. After all, the World is what WE make of it—isn't it? Hey, you didn't really think the world got this way all by itself, did you? Come December 21, 2012, I am going to be in my favorite spot in the whole world: Palenque, Mexico. I will be celebrating the end of it all—the tall tale about 2012 that is. I won't be sitting at home armed to protect my ten-year supply of food stored in the basement. I won't be in a bomb shelter waiting out the end of an age. I am going to be cerebrating the new age and creating paradise, because *I can*—and *you can*, too. Will you join me?

A Way to Live in Peace

In Mayan tradition, there is a greeting that many people working with Mayan wisdom know of. It is the law of In Lak'ech Ala K'in, which means 'I am another yourself' (A modern day interpretation). It also means 'I am you, and you are me' (A traditional Mayan interpretation). We have come to understand that this Mayan greeting is an honoring for each other. It is a statement of unity and oneness. In Lak'ech Ala K'in mirrors the same sentiment of other beautiful greetings, such as Namaste for East India, Wiracocha for the Inca, and Mitakuye Oyasin for the Lakota. It doesn't matter which culture you come from. But when one of these sacred greetings is given, there is always an action of placing the hands over the heart.

The more I walk the Mayan path, the more I understand the depth that In Lak'ech Ala K'in teaches. This greeting has become more than a simple, honorable Maya greeting. It has evolved into a moral code, and a way to create a positive reality for all life. As we near 2012, with all its doom and gloom prophecies, we have a moral obligation to Spirit to live the code of In Lak'ech Ala K'in.

It is common knowledge these days that every action we take in our lives affects all living things. We understand that if we act negatively, our actions impact all life negatively. When we act positively, we affect all life in a positive manner. When we live the Mayan code of In Lak'ech Ala K'in, we know that every action we take is out of respect for all life, and we are living and giving from our hearts.

We can give our hearts in a positive manner every day by saying In Lak'ech Ala K'in to each other, to the trees, to the sky, to the birds, and to the stars. You can greet each sunrise by saying In Lak'ech Ala K'in. Each and every day we have together is sacred, so acknowledge this day by giving it your heart. Remember when you give in this way, you are also giving to yourself! You are not giving your energy away to something separate from yourself. You are giving to another part of yourself!

I understand the challenges in staying positive in these days, where the energy is so compressed that we can hardly breathe, but there is one simple exercise that can turn it all around for us. Each day, simply walk in gratefulness. We can say In Lak'ech Ala K'in to that which gives us life every day, and that is the heart of the Great Spirit. Instead of solely taking from the Great Spirit by asking for insight and direction, give back your heart, love, and appreciation. You will be amazed at the results. If we open our hearts and send gratitude, it opens all doors that were previously closed to us. Remember you are a part of Great Spirit! When you give to Great Spirit you are giving to yourself. We can practice In Lak'ech Ala K'in tirelessly, because when and what we give to others is giving energy to ourselves. When we give, we receive.

So how do we know if we giving right? It is really simple. When energized by giving, we know we are giving from our hearts and from the code of In Lak'ech Ala K'in. If we feel drained or exhausted, it is possible that we gave out of fear, lack, obligation, ego, or a need to be accepted or liked. The more one practices In Lak'ech Ala K'in, the clearer we will become about our motivations regarding our actions, and the more we will receive. Remember, what goes around comes around, exactly the way it was sent out. If you don't like what life is sending to you, look at what you are sending out to life.

When we begin to live and practice In Lak'ech Ala K'in, a lot of our old ways of doing things will no longer work for us. For instance, we cannot act like victims anymore, and we cannot live out of fear either. We find ourselves no longer preparing for disaster; instead, we anticipate a glorious future. It is time for us to rewrite the prophecies. They have become obsolete. The past will become just a bad dream, and the future will become a beautiful vision of which we will create right now. When we practice In Lak'ech Ala K'in, we quit being neutral in our world, because we understand that Spirit works with those that take action. We begin to take action by adding to the positive experience of this dimension. So what kind of world do you want? Don't just stand there waiting for the world to appear in front of you. Spirit helps those who help themselves. It is up to us.

When we practice the moral code of In Lak'ech Ala K'in, we are producing and sending positive and vital energy that can literally transform our troubled world into Paradise. When we live from In Lak'ech Ala K'in, we are putting our natural ability to create our reality to use. We are affecting the collective consciousness of humanity in a positive way. The Cosmic Maya, also known as the 'Star Elders' or 'Invisible Council', understood this natural power to create their reality. Their sacred calendars mapped the natural laws of the universe. Now it is our turn to come to this understanding. It is time for us to walk as the Star Elders did so many years ago. The time has come for us to change the world.

The more humanity begins to live In Lak'ech Ala K'in, the less we will think in terms of our separateness. There can be no competition, jealousy or envy between us, because we are pieces of each other. We can share and help each other with our connections, ideas and resources without fear that there will not be enough to go around. When we live the reality of unity, abundance and wholeness, there will be unity, abundance and wholeness! The more of us that participate in the creation of a better world, the quicker it will arrive. We will have peace, love, harmony and unity, and will finally have arrived home.

Jim Young's Website

www.creationspirit.net contains additional creations to come through Jim Young, including E-books, free downloads, and a link to his collector quality photography. Speaking services and classes dealing with his writings are also available. Contact 1andrea.thomas@gmail.com to arrange an event.

Books by Jim Young

(See **www.creationspirit.net** for descriptions)

Living an Extraordinary Life in an Ordinary Reality (O-Books, Spring 2011)
2013! The Beginning is Here (O-Books)
Aware in a World Asleep (O-Books)
God's Pocket Dictionary
As if from God
On Making Love: Spiritual Testimony to the Gift Life Is
Real Life Leadership in a Newfangled World: The Essential Remedy for a Symptomatic Society
What If...? Changing Your Life to Fit Your Truth
Consider the Source: Rising Above Illusion Into the Light of Truth
Only Mind Matters: Emerging From the Waters of Symbolic Meaning
Keys to the Door of Truth
A Labor of Love: Weaving Your Own Virgin Birth on the Loom of Love
Creation Spirit: Expressing Your Divinity in Everyday Life

BOOKS

O is a symbol of the world, of oneness and unity. In different cultures it also means the "eye," symbolizing knowledge and insight. We aim to publish books that are accessible, constructive and that challenge accepted opinion, both that of academia and the "moral majority."

Our books are available in all good English language bookstores worldwide. If you don't see the book on the shelves ask the bookstore to order it for you, quoting the ISBN number and title. Alternatively you can order online (all major online retail sites carry our titles) or contact the distributor in the relevant country, listed on the copyright page.

See our website **www.o-books.net** for a full list of over 500 titles, growing by 100 a year.

And tune in to myspiritradio.com for our book review radio show, hosted by June-Elleni Laine, where you can listen to the authors discussing their books.

MySpiritRadio